Miracles Made Easy

Claim Your Power
Create Desired Results

Ann McGill

Copyright @ 2008 Ann McGill

This work is licensed under a Creative Commons Attribution-Noncommercial-No Derivative Works 3.0 Unported License described at http://creativecommons.org/licenses/by-nc-nd/3.0/ and further at http://creativecommons.org/licenses/by-nc-nd/3.0/legalcode

You are free to Share — to copy, distribute and transmit the work under the following conditions:

Attribution. You must attribute the work to Ann McGill, Author, *Miracles Made Easy* (but not in any way that suggests that she endorses you or your use of the work).

Noncommercial. You may not use this work for commercial purposes.

No Derivative Works. You may not alter, transform, or build upon this work.

Nothing in this license impairs or restricts the author's moral rights.

For any reuse or distribution, you must make clear to others the license terms of this work by including this entire notice, including a link to the following web page: http://creativecommons.org/licenses/by-nc-nd/3.0/

Any of the above conditions can be waived if you get written permission from the copyright holder, Ann McGill.

First Printing – March 2008
Second Printing – June 2008

Cover and Book Design: Carol Hansen Grey, CustomDynamic.net
Published by Mak-A-Dif Press
ISBN 978-0-9816096-0-7
Library of Congress Control Number: 2008902144
Printed in the United States of America

DEDICATION

Miracles Made Easy is dedicated to all who serve as teachers, mentors and guides in the process of self-discovery and spiritual awakening.

Miracles Made Easy is dedicated to all who open their minds and hearts to receive these gifts and pass them on.

Together we are co-creating an ever more wonderful world.

GRATITUDE

How fortunate the mother with talented daughters committed to helping her convert exciting ideas into a published book. Daughter Megan McGill designed the original logo and created the first prototype book, encouraging me with her enthusiasm to keep on writing. Daughter Amanda Lopez pulled *Miracles Made Easy* out of the file drawer, where it had been languishing for several years, and edited out what was extraneous. Her suggestion to add the "Try This" Experiments transformed a series of interesting tales into a valuable tool.

How fortunate the writer who is supported by a supremely talented "Book Doctor" like Sarah Snyder. Her understanding of metaphysics and spirituality truly enabled me to do my exquisite best, just as Holy Spirit asked. Working together was a truly enjoyable experience.

How fortunate the author who finds a wonderful Graphic Artist to visually convey the essence of their message. Carol Hansen Grey created the book cover and feather logo and then went on to design the book interior. Such fun to dance with such a creative and capable Soul Sister.

How fortunate the individual who learns how marvelously miraculous life can be when we are willing to claim our power and believe in possibilities. I am grateful to the Mystery that sent me teachers like Cynthia, David and Al, and their generosity in sharing what they had learned.

TABLE OF CONTENTS

Preface: How to Get the Most Out of This Book   i

Section One: Foundation   1
- What – Who – Why 3
- Invitation 5
- Creating Context 7
- What to Expect 9
- Experiments in Living™ 11
- Experiments in Living™ Guidelines 13

Section Two: Feather Stories   17
1. *That Makes Sense* 19
   Creating Parking Places
2. *Can I Do That?* 23
   Dissolving Clouds
3. *The Magic of Findhorn* 27
   Energizing with Love
4. *The Woman Got Her Man* 31
   Affirming Desired Results
5. *A Thousand-to-One Shot* 35
   Perfection is Possible
6. *A Free Vacation* 39
   Trusting the Universe
7. *Butterflies Were My Teachers* 43
   Interpreting Signs and Signals
8. *The Well-Aimed Raindrop* 47
   Paying Attention
9. *Rental Units Were Mighty Scarce* 51
   Trusting Guidance
10. *The Baby Needed Milk* 55
    Flowing With Life
11. *I Never Saw the Red Light* 59
    Trusting Your Experience
12. *I'd Been Doing It All Along* 63
    Healing Hands

13. A Field Full of Feathers 69
   Overcoming Fear and Doubt

14. Lesson Learned.. 77
   Waiting Until the Appropriate Moment

15. What Am I to Believe? 83
   One, Two, Three

Section III   Universal Principles   87
- How the Universe Works 89
- Truth 90
- Energy 91
- Thought 92
- Attitude 93
- Learning 94
- Answers 95
- Creating 96
- Bottom Line Message 97

Section IV   Tithing Experiment   99
- Preface Revisited 101
- Now is the Time 102
- Why Tithe 103
- Key Points 104
- Experiment Explained... 105
- Whatever Happens, I've Been Blessed 106

Section V: Next Steps   107
- Share Your Stories 109
- Continue Exploring 110

Appendices   111
A: Tithing – A Way of Life 113
B: Highly Recommended Books 117
C: Highly Recommended Spiritual Teachers 119
D: Highly Recommended Service Providers 121

About Ann McGill 124
Contact Information 124

PREFACE

How to Get the Most out of This Book

Price Builds Credibility

It is human nature to assume that the more something costs, the greater its value. We presume a product's ingredients or quality of workmanship are superior if we pay more. We expect greater knowledge and experience from the consultant with the highest fees. Marketing mavens long ago learned that price builds credibility.

In a similar vein, we tend to distrust or undervalue what is given away for free. Worse yet, lack of upfront investment undermines people's normal motivation to take full advantage and get their money's worth.

Examples of Principles

When Transcendental Meditation was first introduced in America, it was offered for free. There were few takers. Once they started charging $250, its popularity spread rapidly.

Numerous therapists and other service providers have learned through personal experience that clients who receive their services for free, or at much reduced rates, rarely benefit to the same degree as those who are charged an appropriate amount.

Quandary

My purpose in writing *Miracles Made Easy* is to pass on what I consider valuable, essential information. Once enough of us know how to create miracles, we'll collectively have the ability to create a far safer, saner, healthier, happier world. The sooner there are more of us, the faster desired improvements will occur.

Since I want to live in this better world that's truly possible, it behooves me to contribute to its coming into being. This is why I chose to make *Miracles Made Easy* totally affordable and super easy to pass. This is why I am giving the book away for free (anyone can download it at www.MiraclesMadeEasy.com), and am forgoing making a profit on the paperback version (which reduces the price I need to charge.)

This decision, obviously, caused quite a quandary, since it conflicts with people's tendency to devalue what they don't pay top dollar for. By trying to do the world a favor, I would be doing a disservice to you. How could this handicap be overcome? This question had to be answered for readers to obtain maximum benefit.

You'll learn in Section IV, *Tithing Experiment*, the thinking that led to the solution of this dilemma. For the moment, here's what I suggest.

Create Your Own Value

Declare ahead of time what it would be worth to you to learn how to make miracles happen, or to reinforce and expand what you already know: $5-10, $50-100, $1,000 or more. Name an amount you can reasonably afford. Clearly, the higher the monetary value the greater the benefits you can expect to reap.

Read the first ten pages first, if you want to clarify how *Miracles Made Easy* might serve you before stating your intention.

Write this figure down. You can write it here $_____ or better yet, create a bookmark with the amount written across the top. This will remind you of the value you have chosen to receive every time you pick the book back up to read again.

Section One

FOUNDATION

What – Who – Why

Miracles Made Easy is …

… a spiritual primer

for those who want to discover the power of belief and the power of thought to make miracles happen as everyday events.

… a powerful review of principles

for those who want a reminder about how the world really works, and how to make it work better for themselves.

… a doubt-buster

for those who find it difficult to believe the Universal Truths to which they are exposed.

… a how-to guide to manifesting

for those who want tips and techniques, stories with examples and experiments to try.

Invitation

Do you know how to create parking places? What about manifesting the perfect home? Have you ever tried to heal someone with your hands?

What I'm really asking is: Do you know how to make miracles happen – both major and minor –whenever you please, as everyday events?

Miracles Made Easy invites you to join in an exciting journey of discovery. It's an opportunity to learn about the Universal Principles that guide all life, and how to use them to create the life you want. Instead of telling you what to believe with long explanations why, I tell you a story and then describe an experiment you can conduct to prove to yourself what's truly possible.

May your journey of self-discovery be as joyous, illuminating and transforming as mine has been – and continues to be.

Ann McGill
March 2008

Creating Context

Miracles Made Easy describes my explorations into a different kind of everyday reality, and how I came to realize a new personal power.

What caused me to embark upon such a radical journey of self-discovery? You could say I had no choice. A bad case of burnout had sent me to bed for two years and made it impossible to work for two more. My life was a mess. My children were paying the price.

In the early 1980s, a slew of brand new ideas came to my attention. Many seemed strange and far out. I couldn't help noticing how the people espousing these unusual ways of thinking were much happier and more content than anyone I knew. It seemed obvious to me they knew something I didn't, because my life certainly wasn't working well, nor had it been for quite some time. I wanted what they seemed to have – to know more about what they were learning.

That's when I made a commitment that, for the next three months, I would explore as many new ideas as possible and "act as if" all these new ideas were true and actually worked.

Halfway into one of my first *Experiments in Living*™, I realized my life was rapidly, radically changing. While I didn't know where I was going, I definitely knew I wanted to get there. I was led to conclusions that shook my thinking... and they looked promising! It was as if once I had put my foot on this new path, *whoosh!*, more gifts continued to show up.

Lots of teachers came into my life in rapid succession. Many had long been on the spiritual path. With every meeting and conversation, I learned something new.

In the beginning, and for a long time after, much seemed foreign, even weird. I had difficulty fully grasping many of the new concepts to which I was being exposed. What mattered, however, were the results. Much of this new thinking stuck. Over time, clearer explanations and better understandings evolved. Now, many years later, I am living proof that these ideas can have a tremendous constructive impact. It's my hope and intention that you have a similarly powerful, positive experience.

What to Expect

Miracles Made Easy demonstrates the Power of Belief and the Power of Thought to create desired results.

Beliefs form the foundation of who we think we are and how we view the world. When our beliefs are based on misinformation and faulty assumptions, it makes it impossible to find truly viable solutions or to achieve what's potentially possible.

Thoughts are the precursors to the actions we take. Positive thinking empowers, negative thinking undermines. By changing what we think about ourselves and the world around us, we change the outcomes we create.

Section I lays the groundwork that will enable you to get the most out of the stories you read. It introduces *Experiments in Living*™ and describes how to conduct your own explorations for best results.

Section II, the heart of the book, contains a series of what I call my Feather Stories. Each as-I-lived-it teaching tale demonstrates a different principle about how to create what you want in life. Each story includes an experiment you can try so you, too, can experience what's truly possible.

Section III summarizes and reinforces these principles in a way that adds new understanding to the various Feather Stories.

Section IV introduces the principle of Tithing and describes an experiment in which you can participate.

Section V offers suggestions about what you might do next to continue your journey of exploration and self-discovery.

The Appendices are filled with lists of resources readily available to guide and support your journey.

The last pages include the Dedication, Gratitude to those who have most contributed and information about Ann McGill.

Experiments in Living™

Experiments in Living™ are agreements with one's self to explore new ways of thinking, believing and behaving for a specified, limited period of time. It creates opportunities to step out of a rut, see things differently, discover new truths and create more satisfying results.

For the life of the experiment, you agree to release all skepticism, suspend all judgment and temporarily "act as if" a new belief or way of doing things is true and valid. When you refuse to allow fear, doubt and worry to dictate your actions, you open your mind to new possibilities and a more accurate understanding of Truth.

One time I wondered what would happen if I did only what I wanted to for two weeks. I found myself napping twice a day and eating ice cream for breakfast, lunch and dinner. The experiment made me realize just how tired I had been, how much more sleep I really needed. Indulging my inner kid's love for ice cream was great fun, and I was glad to discover that my rampant desire to indulge had significantly diminished by the end of the experiment!

The most profound experiment I ever conducted totally turned my life around. I was converted from doubting skeptic to grateful believer, from avowed agnostic to student of the spiritual. Learning how to make mini-miracles happen as everyday events transformed me from disempowered victim into a proactive creator.

Since this book was written, I've conducted other "I-wonder-what-if..." explorations: rising at 4:30 in the morning; doing without television; giving money to strangers; putting a smile on my face, even when I didn't feel like it; assuming there was a good reason behind receiving "bad" news; "acting as if" a person who bothered me really did have my best interests at heart.

Miracles Made Easy describes what began as a three-month experiment and grew into a way of life. The experiments enabled me to discover that life works quite differently from what I had always thought, and showed me how I could make my life work better. Here's what I did.

I tried on every idea and belief that I was exposed to concerning spirituality and metaphysics, no matter how outlandish or far out it seemed. I "acted as if" everything I had heard was true, and waited until the results of my experiments were in to decide what I actually believed.

I committed to being as pro-active as possible during the experimental period, knowing that anything less wouldn't do. I wanted to discover what was possible, and these metaphysical ideas were new to me.

This attitude and approach will enable you to create the most positive results possible. Following are some suggestions that have served me well as I conducted various experiments.

Experiments in Living™ Guidelines

- **Decide what your experiment will be.**

    What do you want to know? What are you curious about? What would you like to prove – to yourself – does or doesn't work? You want to pick something that challenges your thought patterns, changes the way you normally do things. Know that it sometimes takes courage to test the boundaries of our comfort zone.

- **Determine when the experiment will begin and how long it will last.**

    Pick a time when you can pay attention and not be pulled off course by people or other distractions. For instance, you might not want to experiment at getting up at 4:30 in the morning the weekend you visit your night-owl parents.

    The time frame needs to be long enough to allow newness to unfold so answers can reveal themselves. You might need only a couple of days to see what it's like to go without speaking a single swear word. But you'll certainly need several months to discover whether or not your spouse's behavior changes when you thank him every time he criticizes you.

- **Never commit to more than three months at a time.**

    This drops in place a safety precaution to keep you from getting too far off track, pursuing directions that are not healthy or fruitful. If the experiment needs more time to properly unfold, you can always re-up for another three months.

- **Agree to set aside all fear and worry for the stated period of time.**

    This is essential. Should second thoughts arise – and they often do – remind yourself of your commitment to look at any concerns that crop up later, not during the experiment.

    Maybe you decide to create more free time by cutting back at work. Any time your inner voice begins to chatter – *this was a big mistake; my job's in jeopardy; my co-workers are getting upset* – remind yourself quite forcefully that you've already determined it is safe to temporarily slow down. Ignore the fear talk until the experiment is over.

    Naturally, if your situation should significantly change – your company is sold or you get a new boss – then you might consider postponing the experiment until you can give it the time and attention it deserves.

- **Keep an open mind.**

    You can't learn anything new and valuable if you think you already know the answers. Focus on gathering information, not on the conclusions you're likely draw. If you find yourself assuming, appraising, expecting and judging, remind yourself that curiosity opens the mind to greater truths.

    Remember, we see what we believe, get what we expect and are unlikely to experience what we assume to be impossible.

- **Be prepared – willing – to get upset, to feel lost and confused.**

    Perhaps you'll undergo a major shift in consciousness, as happened to me. Maybe your understanding of how the world works will be forever, fundamentally, changed. It can be quite disconcerting to have our foundations rattled, our belief systems turned upside down.

    If this should happen to you, remember, the disruption is only temporary. You will soon stabilize in a new world view that will serve you ever so much better. Reach out and talk to someone who's been there and who understands what is happening to you.

- **Journal about the process.**

    Once you've written something down, it becomes difficult to deny that you've actually thought it. Journaling helps clarify thinking and strengthen observations. Rereading about your experience can trigger fresh insights and suggest new directions to pursue.

- **At the end of the experiment, stop and assess.**

    What have you learned? What did you experience? How might your beliefs have changed? Do you see things differently? Do these new ideas still need proving? Do they hold promise?

    If you decide to continue, state the amount of additional time you'll give to your quest, but don't exceed three months. Just as before, stop and assess again.

- **Share your experience.**

    Speaking our experience aloud reinforces new learnings. People's questions and comments encourage us to explore more deeply. Your stories offer family and friends the opportunity to benefit from your experiments and explorations.

Section Two

FEATHER STORIES

ONE

That Makes Sense: Creating Parking Places
More Traffic, Fewer Spaces

One of the chronic frustrations of driving in urban areas is the paucity of places to park. Wouldn't it be wonderful if we could create a parking space whenever we needed one?

When I was a sales executive for Xerox Corporation, my manager told me how he always found a place to park right up close to where he was going. Since finding parking can be a major difficulty for sales people, the idea of ready and waiting parking places appealed to me. Here's how Gary explained his inordinate good luck.

"Think about it, Ann. Most people grab the first empty space they see, for fear of not finding another one that's closer. This leaves the nearer spaces free. It's human nature to hang on to what we've got when there's no guarantee of getting something better." I saw his point.

"I do quite the opposite," Gary continued. "I don't start looking until I get to where I'm going. Most of the time, there's a convenient space right near the front door. Or, just as I arrive, someone pulls out." I could see that it was logic, not luck, that Gary was talking about.

Creating Good Fortune

By refusing to assume the worst, Gary created his own good fortune. Statistically, he increased the likelihood of finding a convenient parking place by being willing to look for it, to assume that one was probably available.

I recalled times when I had trudged in from some distant spot, only to pass empty spaces closer in. I knew that if I tried Gary's method and it didn't work, I'd be no worse off than if I hadn't bothered. If Gary could do it, I could too!

That's when I began driving right up to the entrance of a building before I even started looking for a place to park. I was delighted when open spaces appeared with surprising frequency.

Sharing what I'd learned and the results I was experiencing with my teenage daughters, they enthusiastically joined the game. Our successes grew. As we'd set off for the shopping mall on a busy Saturday, they, too, held the positive thought that we'd find a close-in space to park. No more long walks across huge parking lots for this family. The worse the weather, the more we appreciated our new-found ability.

By suspending my doubts and trying on new beliefs, I changed my fortune. The more parking places I found – or dare I say "created" – the more I confirmed Gary's logic. It was not until later that I learned the underlying lesson that Gary had inadvertently taught me: What we think is what we get. We have the power to create whatever reality we want.

As you've likely heard before, *experience is the best teacher*. Reading about something, or intellectually understanding it, doesn't prove a thing. Firsthand experience, however, can't be denied. So of course, I suggest you "Try This" yourself.

Try This

- Envision your destination and where you want to park. If imagery doesn't work easily for you, describe your intention in words; for example, within a block in any direction, or on the south side of the lake.

- As you drive to wherever you're headed, expect to find a parking space as requested. If one doesn't appear, assume there is a good reason. Maybe a handicapped person needs the space that's about to open up, or you really could use the exercise by walking farther. This step is important. You'll learn why when we talk about feathers and acceptance.

- Don't draw conclusions when you fail to create the parking space you wanted. It doesn't prove a thing. Since *what you focus on expands* (e.g., pain worsens when we pay attention to it), the more you focus on negative experiences, the more they're likely to occur. Instead, choose to notice with glee every time you successfully create a perfect close-in spot. Reinforcement of positive outcomes strengthens belief in new possibilities.

TWO

Can I Do That?
Dissolving Clouds

Belief Without Proof

Wayne Dyer's book *You'll See It When You Believe It* describes how our scientifically oriented way of thinking makes us demand absolute tangible evidence before we believe in something new. This way of thinking is summarized by the erroneous age-old adage "I'll believe it when I see it."

A good example of such knee-jerk refusal to believe what can't be seen is Western medicine's long-standing rejection of what has been a key element of Chinese medicine for thousands of years. I'm referring to the existence of auras (energy fields that surround the body) and *chi* (energy that courses through the body). Only in the past decade has acupuncture (which releases blocked energy) become increasingly accepted as a valuable healing modality in the West.

What's so interesting about human nature is our basic unwillingness to challenge and change historical thinking, even when science proves otherwise. Based on Kirlian photography, photographing auras is a prime example. The process, popularized in the 1970s, captures auras on film to "prove" their existence. Yet many in the Western medical community reject the existence of auras and *chi*. Sometimes our beliefs are so strong that we won't consider new evidence that might cause us to see things differently.

Wanting irrefutable proof for new concepts that we don't understand or think unbelievable, we tend to forget how much of life we take on faith, without proof. We can't see electricity yet we firmly believe in its existence. We can't see radio waves and X-rays, yet we use them every day. You can see why I predict that one day acceptance of *chi* and auras will be equally unquestioned.

Making Clouds Disappear

When I was first learning about *chi* and auras, I read about a man who could make clouds disappear at will. Because the author had been so convincing about other things up until this part of his story, I chose to believe this rather dubious tale about trying to make clouds disappear. Although the author didn't describe how the man did it, I decided to try it myself anyway.

My first attempt at dissolving clouds was during a long drive home from North Carolina to Virginia. The day was beautiful and bright with puffy pockets of white fluff hanging in an otherwise clear blue sky. Not wanting to fail, I picked one of the smallest puff balls I could find. I simply stared at my chosen cloud as best I could. The wee bit of cloud was soon no more.

Beyond My Experience

Figuring I must have picked a wisp that was ready to dissolve anyway, I tried again. This time I chose a slightly larger cloud, focusing on a frayed edge. I pretended my eyes were sending laser-like beams of intense energy that had the power to melt and dissolve. Within five minutes, the cloud started to get smaller, and soon it disappeared altogether.

My initial reaction was *What a great way to pass time on a long trip!* My second thought was *But it doesn't prove a thing!*

I still wasn't convinced that I had done what I thought I had. What was apparently happening just wouldn't compute. How could I be the cause? It didn't fit my picture of reality. It was beyond my experience or ability to comprehend. I concluded I needed to try again.

Impossible to Forget

The third time, I selected an even bigger, fatter cloud. It vanished as well. Suddenly, I began to feel extremely anxious. Why it was so disturbing, I couldn't say. I really didn't want to think about it. So I turned on the radio to avoid further consideration.

However, it was impossible to forget the experience. Perhaps it was the high-speed movement of the car that had somehow created the illusion of clouds disappearing. I needed to see if it worked while I remained stationary.

The following week, I went to a nearby park and settled down in my favorite spot. As I lay back and looked up, I saw an inviting blue sky filled with cotton ball clouds. Each was distinct, floating peacefully, going nowhere. Once again, I set out to dissolve a really small puff. I couldn't believe how easy it was. Three clouds dissolved – bing, bing, bang – just like that!

Dissolving clouds still felt like pretty far-out stuff. Despite the evidence, I needed more proof that I had really done the inexplicable. A week later, I tried once more. More clouds disappeared. All I did was relax, believe and concentrate on sending bolts of energy straight from my eyes into the clouds, which simply melted away. It was enough to convince me that I really had made them disappear. It was enough to scare me into stopping again.

Difficult and Dangerous

It felt as if I had been doing something dangerous. I doubted I could do it again. The thought that I could have so much power was scary. If I could dissolve clouds, what other amazing things could I do? Not ready to face the implications of this realization, I stopped exploring and experimenting for quite a long time.

As much as these experiences disturbed me, I had to keep on playing with it. When I finally took up cloud dissolving again, I tried several new techniques. My favorite was thinking of the blue sky as a flat plane with a slit in it. I would insert a cloud as if stuffing an envelope, letting a gentle breeze nudge the cloud forward until it slipped into the opening slice and disappeared behind the sky.

As you explore what works best for you, forget about theoretical explanations about why the clouds dissolve. We often discover more when we know less to begin with. This helps us maintain an open mind. What's important are your own experiences.

Try This

- Wait for a day that isn't windy. Otherwise the clouds can rush by so fast, you might doubt that you made them disappear. Because concentration is key, and bigger clouds take longer to dissolve, choose a small fluff of cumulus for your first attempt. It's best to find a cloud that is neither intimidating nor time consuming.

- Keep in mind there's no right way to do it. There are no skills or techniques to be learned. Feel free to try what worked for me (such as sending a laser beam or stuffing an envelope), or explore your own ideas. What you believe dictates what happens.

- Be sure to thank the clouds for cooperating. It never hurts to express appreciation whenever we get our way, even if it's not a person granting our requests.

THREE

The Magic of Findhorn
Energizing with Love

Forty-pound Cabbages

Shortly after my experience dissolving clouds, someone suggested I read *The Magic of Findhorn*, a true story about a cooperative community founded in 1962 by Eileen and Peter Caddy and Dorothy McClean.

Before Eileen and Peter met, they both began receiving messages from God that led them to meet and marry. Continued guidance took them through a long series of experiences that, in hindsight, seemed designed to prepare them for their life's work. Eventually, their guidance led them to a desolate spit of land off the north coast of Scotland along the North Sea, where they were led to plant flowers and vegetables.

The townspeople considered their plan absurd. Anyone could see what generations of forebears knew: nothing could bloom in such sandy soil or a windswept environment. You can imagine their reaction when Findhorn became world famous for its magnificent gardens and its 40-pound cabbages.

Since reading about Findhorn, I've met a number of people who have seen the gardens and met the founders. They all confirmed that flowers and vegetables typically grow much larger than normal.

We All Have the Ability

The Magic of Findhorn provided several explanations for such extraordinary green-thumbed success. It described how some people can "channel" messages from God, receiving guidance that tells them what to do and new avenues to try. The book also talks about *Devas*, or Nature Spirits, that work directly with growing things.

The *Devas'* advice is accessible to those who learn how to tune in to it. As Findhorn so clearly demonstrates, *Devas* can help us do far more than we can without such assistance. We all have the ability to connect with Mother Nature – God, Spirit, a Power Greater than Ourselves. It's not a talent limited to a chosen few.

Same Seeds, Different Results

The story of Findhorn reminded me of an article I once read about a high school girl's science class experiment. She planted two fields from the same batch of seeds. One received love, the other anger and negativity. One field was treated to kind words and classical music. The other was either ignored or exposed to harsh words and raucous music. Both fields received the same amount of watering and sunlight.

Can you guess what happened? The plants in the positive field grew huge, straight and tall. The plants in the negative field were stunted, withered and blighted. While this high school student knew nothing about Nature Spirits, her experiment demonstrated Findhorn's basic message.

Try This

- Create two gardens or groupings of plants. Keep them physically separated enough so that one group is not affected by how you treat the other. It's essential that they be exposed to the same sunlight, temperature, wind and soil. You can do this experiment with sweet potatoes, which take about six weeks to blossom, or beans, which grow quite rapidly.

- Treat the positive group as you would a best friend. Tell the plants how beautiful they are and how much you appreciate the pleasure they bring to your life. Sing to them songs of joy and gentle lullabies. The more you share your love and happiness, the more your plants will thrive.

- Subject the negative group to loud noise, bad language, rage and anger. Try music with harsh sounds, a bone-jarring beat.

- Record your actions and observations.

FOUR

The Woman Got Her Man
Affirming Desired Results

What Do You Want?

Every time I saw David, he had something new and interesting to share. In addition to creating parking spaces, he told me about affirmations.

"Affirmations are positive statements you frequently repeat about what you want to happen," he said, "stated as if the results have already been achieved. For instance, if you're aim is to lose weight, you might affirm: *I lose weight quickly and easily. I am now at my minimum weight.* Or if you need a new car, you might say: *I am now driving a sporty, new yellow car that is easily affordable.*"

David explained how affirmations work and their power to bring about desired results by telling me a story about Jackie. Divorced for a number of years, Jackie was tired of being single. While she had plenty of dates, what she really wanted was to settle down. Jackie had decided to use affirmations to attract a husband.

Her first step was to think about everything she wanted in a mate. He had to be intelligent with a good sense of humor, taller than 5'10", physically attractive and with a full head of hair.

For Jackie, it was important that her ideal mate share her interest in classical music and prefer books to television. He also had to like children because Jackie's were quite young. Jackie also wanted a good lover, one who enjoyed snuggling and hugging. These traits began a much longer list.

Positive Statements

Next, Jackie turned the list of ideal qualities into a series of positive statements. For example: *I attract a man who is joyful, caring and generous. He loves me and my children deeply. He loves classical music and talking about books. He has a wonderful sense of humor and is sensuous, nurturing and kind.*

She then set a "by-when" date, New Year's Eve of that year, three months hence. She continued dating, but with a more critical eye: *Could this be him? Does he like kids?*

Figuring she'd do what she could to improve the odds of finding her man, Jackie became more active, going to more places where she might meet men: dancing, a week-end workshop, a local comedy club. These activities continued throughout October and November with nary a flutter of interest.

Minutes Before Midnight

Next thing Jackie knew, it was New Year's Eve and Mr. Right had not appeared. Rather than bemoaning her bad luck, or disparaging herself for having trusted the power of affirmations, Jackie headed for the party her friend Michelle was giving. Knowing Michelle, there was a good chance a couple of not-yet-met bachelors would be present.

By 11:45 p.m., Jackie had met every single man at the party. None had generated even the tiniest flutter in her heart to signal he might be the one. Time was nearly up. She would have to accept that the affirmation process didn't work – at least not this time.

Suddenly, there was a knock at the door. In walked a man, neither tall nor short, with dark, curly hair. Not pausing to remove his coat, he made a beeline for Jackie. "Hi, my name is Sam. I can't tell you how surprised I am to be here tonight."

Before Jackie could say more than, "And my name is Jackie," Sam rushed on. "Gosh you look beautiful. As I entered the apartment, it was as if you were the only one in the room. All I could see was you. I just had to meet you."

At his point, Sam hesitantly put his hand to his mouth and gave a little cough. "Before you get a bad impression, I ought to say that I'm not usually this forward."

Jackie didn't mind a bit, especially after finding out he loved kids and classical music.

Creating Desired Reality

Sam was a cello player with an orchestra in Texas, which had just been performing a concert in New York. Michelle had asked him to visit during his layover in Atlanta, but he declined, knowing he would be too tired from all his concerts during the Christmas season. When bad weather grounded his plane overnight in Atlanta, he decided to go to the party after all. That was why he was so late, arriving just minutes before midnight.

Jackie and Sam were immediately enamored with each another. From here, the story unfolded as you might expect – if you believe in the power of affirmations to create desired reality.

Despite their long-distance relationship, Sam and Jackie quickly realized their mutual desire to be lifelong partners. Since she had the more portable career, they decided she would be the one to move. Within six months, they were married and living happily in Texas.

This experience taught Jackie the importance of asking for everything she wanted, in great detail. She had gotten all she requested except for one important item: Jackie had neglected to put on her affirmation list that the man of her dreams would live in her beloved Atlanta.

If we don't tell the Universe exactly what we want, how can it know exactly what to give us?

Try This

- Make a list of what you want. Describe it in detail. Make sure you've included everything important. Then set a date by when you want to receive what you've asked for.

- Convert your desire into positive affirmations. Avoid being negative. Instead of saying *He's not too short*, try *He's at least two inches taller than me.* Use exciting descriptive adjectives: *My perfect mate loves and adores me. He's a fabulous dancer and a divine cook.* Replace *My future husband is willing to help around the house* with *He cheerfully helps keep our household running smoothly.*

- Repeat the affirmations 10 times daily. Speaking affirmations out loud and writing them down strengthens their power, for the information is now being processed physically and physiologically, as well as mentally and emotionally.

- Make it easier for the Universe to respond to your request by taking appropriate actions to support your affirmations. If you want a partner, don't stay at home. Attend a lecture, a concert, a class reunion. Sign up for a workshop, take dancing lessons, go on vacation.

- Remember, the more you believe affirmations actually work, and the more you believe you deserve to get what you want, the greater the likelihood your desires will manifest.

FIVE

A Thousand-to-One Shot
Perfection Is Possible

Speaking Into Being

Affirmations are a powerful tool for reprogramming the unconscious mind. They can help us change undermining beliefs and strengthen intentions. Affirmations make clear, to ourselves and the Universe, what we most want. They inject energy into our everyday thoughts.

When my friend David first learned about affirmations, he and his wife, Joan, wanted to buy a new house. They found one they particularly liked being sold by raffle for $100 a ticket. This seemed like a good opportunity to test affirmation theory, so they took a chance.

David and Joan agreed to write their affirmations daily until the drawing: *Ticket number 1234 wins. We now own a beautiful, brand new home on Cherry Wood Lane.* Later, David admitted he had gotten bored with all that writing so simply spoke them aloud as he drove around doing his real estate business.

Before the raffle date, the house owner called to say it had been canceled; not enough people had purchased tickets. However, if they wanted, they could convert their $100 ticket into two $50 chances on the money that had been collected. They agreed to continue, and amended their affirmation accordingly: *Ticket number 1234 is selected. Ticket number 9876 wins.*

When the owner called again, it was to say, "I've got wonderful news. You've won the first-place prize! Congratulations!" Of course, David and Joan were thrilled.

"And," the man continued, "you won second place as well!" This happy couple didn't know whether to be more excited about winning so much money or for having just proved just how powerful affirmations can be.

This or Something Better

Whether praying or affirming, whenever we ask for what we want, it can be a good idea to add the phrase, "This or something better" as the last part of your affirmation. Because we often lack the big-picture, long-term perspective, this added statement is a way to acknowledge that later we might not want what we're asking for.

Two years after winning the raffle, Joan and David unexpectedly divorced, after 22 years of marriage. By winning the cash instead of the house, they avoided the expense and stress of moving into a new house, which they later would have had to sell. Instead, the Universe gave them something better – cash – which is easier to divide than a house. As the saying goes, "Everything is always in perfect, divine order."

Try This

- Identify exactly what you want to manifest. Write appropriate affirmations. Declare when you want it to happen. Either state a specific date, or say something like *during the year 200X* or *before the end of summer this year*.

- Imagine having what you want. Mentally and emotionally enjoy the experience of spending the money, seeing yourself living in the new house, hearing yourself being congratulated. The more detailed your imaginary experience, and the more senses you employ, the greater the positive energy field created to help you attract what you seek.

- Speak and write your affirmations daily, or at least frequently. Repetition strengthens the signal sent to your subconscious and to the Universe itself.

- The more you trust and believe it will happen, the better your chances of receiving your heart's desires. Remember, negative thoughts interfere with any positive energy you are building to attract what you want. This was the lesson of the plant experiment in Story 3.

- Be sure to say "thank you" for the support and assistance received. Thank all those involved, human, Spirit and Nature. And if things don't turn out as requested and expected, remember, at some future date, you may be glad!

SIX

A Free Vacation
Trusting the Universe

A Lesson in Metaphysics

Early in the exploration process, I visited a psychic for the very first time. I had no idea what to expect and was amazed by the reading. Knowing little more than my name and birth date, Cynthia talked for more than an hour, telling me things about myself and my past that she had no way of knowing unless she were me.

She said something that really caught my attention: "Ann, you feel as if you've just been through your own World War III." I considered this an apt description of what I had experienced the previous few years.

"If I could make a wish for you," Cynthia continued, "it would be that you take a relaxing vacation for at least two weeks." She then taught me one of my very first lessons in metaphysics: "Every dollar you spend to help yourself heal and mend will be replaced. You can count on it."

Taking a Vacation

Since I had committed to trying on other people's belief systems, I took her advice. Deep down, I knew she was right. I really did need to get out of town and take a break from all life's pressures. The following week, I consulted a travel agent and planned a marvelous sailing trip in the Bahamas.

What you need to know is that I couldn't afford it. My savings were all used up and my retirement fund was spent. I had only enough money in the bank to keep me afloat for several more months, and I knew it would be quite a while before I'd be strong enough to work again. I was nearly tapped out financially. This time, I was definitely testing my *Experiments in Living*™ commitment. I spent a third of what I had and went on vacation.

Cynthia was oh so right! After two weeks of swimming, sunning, sailing and sleeping – two weeks free of reminders about my desperate plight – I felt like a new woman. I could think clearly, accomplish more and do it better. My attitude improved tremendously. I felt more hopeful, confident and capable than I had felt in a long time.

Trusting the Universe

As I sorted through the mail upon my first night home, a letter from my accountant caught my attention. Why was he writing? My business had long been shut down, and I hadn't seen him in more than a year.

> *Dear Ann,*
>
> *Enclosed is a $1,200 tax refund. We submitted a request in your name based on income averaging for the past five years. Hope it helps.*

It did. It paid for more than half of my trip. A couple of days later, I found this in my mailbox:

> *Dear Ann,*
>
> *I trust your vacation gave you the rest you needed. Wish I could do more, but maybe the enclosed check will help.*
>
> *Love, Mother*

The amount was just enough to pay for the rest of my vacation. It was the first time my mother had ever sent me money out of the blue. Hmm. Makes you wonder, doesn't it? It certainly caught my attention.

I remembered what my knowledgeable psychic had said: *Every dollar you spend to help yourself heal and mend will be replaced. You can count on it!* I believed Cynthia and acted on her advice. Her prediction had come true. When I trusted the Universe and Life, I was supported.

This same principle applies not just to regaining your health, but to getting a job, creating greater peace and satisfaction or doing whatever is important for your basic well being.

Try This

- What do you really need but think you cannot afford? I'm not talking about being foolish and running up credit card debt on things you truly can do without. This experiment is about the Universe supporting those who are helping themselves, not indulging themselves.

- If you find it difficult to spend money on yourself, consider smaller treats, like taking yourself out to dinner, buying some uplifting music or replacing that old shower curtain with something bright and cheery. Do something you wouldn't normally do. Step out of your comfort zone of how it's always been.

- Remember, it's important to believe with all your might that you will be supported. Then be sure to pay attention to what happens afterward. Be aware that it may not be money you receive to replace what you've spent. Maybe a friend offers to fix your car, saving you from having to pay a repair bill. Maybe your dry-cleaner ruins your dress and writes you a check to replace it. Maybe you never really liked that dress and decide to find something new for half the price.

SEVEN

Butterflies Were My Teachers
Interpreting Signs and Signals

Conduits of Information

This chapter introduces the subject of guidance. One way to receive guidance is through symbolic signs and signals. Like the detective Sherlock Holmes, we must not only be good at deciphering the meaning of such clues, but be aware that they exist in the first place.

At the beginning of my journey, I had been told that cars can serve as conduits for messages of advice and guidance from the Universe. I later learned that this applies to other machines as well, such as dishwashers and computers. For example, let's say you run out of gas. Besides indicating forgetfulness or negligence, it might mean that you, yourself, are low on fuel. Maybe you lack sufficient energy to do what you need. Are you getting enough protein, exercise, sleep?

If you get a flat tire, you might want to ask, "How am I lacking the support I need? What's slowing me down? Where am I wasting energy? Have I been ignoring that I'll soon be flat broke?

Your Inner Knowing

As you play detective and analyze what's happening, "as if" it is a symbolic message meant just for you, keep in mind there is no "right" answer. Whatever your interpretation, it will likely produce some fruitful thinking.

Just as no one can accurately analyze a dream for you, no one can tell you what a sign might mean. But peoples' suggestions can be mighty helpful or right on target. Only your gut instinct can tell you whether something you or someone else suggests truly applies to your life and situation. What we're talking about here is intuitive insight, learning to trust your inner knowing, your instinctive interpretive skills.

When I first learned about guidance and trusting my intuition, the Universe chose a method of teaching that was interesting and offbeat. While this story may seem silly, all I can do is report how my own personal belief system unfolded.

Listening to Butterflies

After several years spent mostly in bed, I began to regain my health and stamina, which allowed me to spend a great deal of time at a beautiful nearby park. I found walking in nature, listening to the birds and watching the squirrels to be nurturing and healing.

Sometimes my energy was so low, it sapped all my strength just to hike to a favorite spot. If someone was already there, I'd have to muster all the energy I could just to return to my car and get myself back home to bed.

One day when I was feeling especially poorly, a butterfly flitted in front of my face. A few feet farther along the path, another nearly landed on my nose. So I paused to watch the butterflies dash and flutter about. When I arrived at my favorite spot on the rock overlooking the river, it was occupied. I wasn't relishing the return trek to my car. The next day, I once again headed back to my favorite spot, having missed the pleasure it offered the day before. Again, the butterflies appeared. Again, I stopped to enjoy and admire them. Again, there was someone sitting on my rock.

The third time this happened, I began to wonder about the connection between the butterflies and finding that someone had snagged my spot. Could the butterflies be trying to tell me something? Thinking back, I remembered several occasions when there had been no butterflies, and I had my favorite rock all to myself.

This accumulating evidence led me to recognize a definite pattern. I concluded the butterflies were actually speaking to me through their actions. The days they darted and flitted about in front of my face, they were saying, *Stay away; it'll be a wasted trip.* Their absence indicated *All clear ahead; proceed.*

Thanking the Universe

Several times I double-checked that my interpretation was correct. I ignored the butterflies' warning message to stay away and then wished I hadn't. I soon realized they could be trusted to let me know when someone occupied my special spot.

Without my having asked for support, the Universe assisted me, giving me a sign as a gift. So of course, I thanked the butterflies the next time I saw them. A dose of gratitude never hurt anyone.

A Building Process

Belief is a process of building, incident upon incident. We don't often change our beliefs about things without good reason. First, something usually comes along that challenges our long-held assumptions. Quite often we dismiss the evidence as irrelevant or inconsequential. However, the more we are willing to consider new possibilities, the more difficult it becomes to hang on to old thought patterns.

It is natural to go through a phase of doubting and questioning, and it often lasts quite a long time. Ideally, this grows into a greater willingness to ponder other explanations. The more open minded we are, the more likely we are to draw new conclusions that better explain our experiences and observations.

Try This

- Has anything occurred recently in your life that might be a potential sign or symbol? Ask your gut, your intuition, your Inner Wisdom for suggestions about possible interpretations. Did the postman deliver the wrong mail? Maybe it's time to meet your new neighbor. Did lightning strike a tree that fell a few feet from your house? Maybe it's telling you there's no need to worry about some potentially bad news you just received; it will be a near miss, too.

- Notice if an event keeps repeating itself. If something similar happens three times, that's a sure sign from the Universe to pay attention! Maybe you banged your knee, then hurt your foot and a stray baseball bopped you on the head. It's time to ask what these clues mean. Do you need to slow down, take a break, put your feet up? Are you turning the anger you feel toward your partner inward, punishing yourself instead of addressing the real problem?

  Or maybe you've had a bad-luck run of electrical and mechanical breakdowns. Your tape recorder, phone and email all stopped working within the same week. Realizing these are all related to communicating, you would be wise to wonder in what other areas communication is an issue for you.

- As you explore the signs and signals that provide clues about what to do or what not to pursue, about what you need or how you might be undermining yourself, keep it light. Play it like a game, knowing that it may take time to figure out the "rules" that govern this particular signaling system.

EIGHT

The Well-Aimed Raindrop
Paying Attention

Recognizing the Pattern

Listening and paying attention are essential to receiving guidance and support from the Universe. I had learned about signs and signals from the butterflies. The lesson was further reinforced with raindrops.

One overcast day I sat down at the picnic table to write an article on a new and difficult subject. The sun would peak through periodically then disappear. Soon, a few raindrops fell, forcing me to put away my notebook. Then the sun quickly popped out, so I began writing again.

Ten minutes later, several more raindrops made an inky mess of what I had just written. A few minutes after that, the skies cleared, prompting me to return to my writing. The third time this stop-and-go sequence occurred, I wondered if it was more than mere coincidence.

Rereading what I had written, I realized the raindrops had fallen at the very moment when I had begun digressing from my main point.

For more than an hour, this rain dance continued in which I would write for a while before the rain suggested I take a closer look at what I had written. I noticed these wet-paper signals kept occurring the moment my thinking became fuzzy. While the butterflies had continued sending me messages for six weeks, this was the first and last time raindrops were used as a sign that I was to pay attention.

The 'Aha' Moment

I don't expect this incident to cause the same kind of 'aha' moment for you that it did for me. Rather, my story points out that it is the accumulation of evidence that softens our doubts and resistance. As we open ourselves to new ways of thinking and being, hearing about other peoples' experiences helps us more readily recognize similar events when they happen to us.

The idea is not to persuade ourselves that the Universe is speaking to us, but rather to allow ourselves to discover whether something might be going on that we previously hadn't noticed. It's not about gathering the kinds of concrete proof that will convince us. Because – as the butterflies and raindrops made clear – that often doesn't happen. It's up to you to notice, become aware, ponder possibilities.

Only when we choose to play the Signs and Signals Game of interpreting the seemingly mundane do "minor coincidences" become more meaningful and useful. Pay attention to whatever is unusual, not the norm, as well as the details of an experience: lots of butterflies, more than usual, one nearly landing on my nose; just a few raindrops landing where and when I needed to signal when my writing digressed or needed to be more clear.

 **Try This**

- Unless we set an intention, we're far less likely to achieve our goals. For one week, decide to pay closer-than-usual attention to the events unfolding in your life. Look for repetitive patterns.

- Remember the "Rule of Three." Three of the same, three different but related, is a signal to look deeper. Guess, assess, what the symbolic meaning might be.

- Think back over recent events or scan the past year, to see if you notice any repetitive patterns or signs and signals. We tend to work on issues and new learnings in cycles. Life keeps repeating itself until we get the lesson and try something different. Be aware there is no such thing as coincidence – everything happens for a reason. Be willing to momentarily "act as if" there is significant meaning, for how else can you find out?

- Don't ask these incidents to serve as any kind of proof. Instead, just add them to your accumulating pile of interesting possibilities. If you can't make sense of a particular fluke, happenstance or twist of fate, wait to see if it later becomes part of a larger pattern that makes things more obvious.

- Trust that eventually you will figure out this as-yet-not-defined truth in which you are being asked to believe. This puts you in a state of receptivity, making room for teachers and lessons to show up at the very moment they are most needed and will have the greatest impact. Your open-minded willingness will enable you to recognize the mini-miracles that are part of your daily life. In time, you will discover that these seemingly amazing synchronistic events are actually quite common.

NINE

Rental Units Were Mighty Scarce
Trusting Guidance

Get Busy Affirming

Unable to work for more than two years, nearly out of funds for basic necessities, I decided to sell my house to obtain the monies that would keep me afloat for awhile. The timing wasn't good, for the real estate market was depressed. Fortunately, David, my Realtor, had already taught me about affirmations. He suggested I get busy affirming: *My house sells quickly and easily for a sum very close to my asking price. I quickly find a perfect home to rent that is easily affordable.* My house sold within weeks for close to my asking price, despite the fact it was in poor condition.

David and I immediately started looking at townhouses and apartments for rent that fit my criteria. I definitely wanted to live in the same town, a place I loved. Unfortunately, the vacancy rate at the time was unusually low, just 3%, with almost no turnover in rental property. I had just six weeks to find a new home and move in.

The first place we visited was dirty, dark and dreary. I wanted lots of light. The next two places were also inadequate. One lacked enough bedrooms, another was on a busy street that certainly didn't satisfy my requirement for peace and quiet.

Finally, David showed me a modern house with plenty of windows and overlooking a golf course. While it didn't have everything on my wish list, I loved its looks and location, so I said, "Yes, let's go for it." Five days later, David called to say the landlord wouldn't allow cats. Mine was definitely coming with me. It was back to house hunting again.

The Universe Took Good Care of Me

Despite my seeming bad luck, the Universe was actually taking good care of me. It had heard my detailed requests and evidently wasn't about to let me accept less than what I had asked for. Thanks to the no-pet policy, I avoided renting a place that would have been a second-best choice. It was the fear of running out of time that led me to act hastily.

A few days later, David called to say he had found the perfect house. He was sure I would love it – and I did. It was big and modern, with hardwood floors, and surrounded by trees in a quiet neighborhood. It was everything I had asked for and within my budget. I was excited, eager to sign on the dotted line.

As we descended to the basement to check out where my office would be, David flipped the switch. The light didn't work. "I guess the bulb's burnt out," he said. "I'll go get a flashlight out of the car."

I didn't say a word but thought, *Did the burnt-out lightbulb have significant meaning? Was this a message I needed to pay attention to?*

Heeding the lightbulb's warning, I took David's flashlight and gave the basement a good looking over. That was when I noticed it had only one small window high up, which wouldn't provide the daylight I required for my office. This was bad news. I sighed in gratitude for the flash of insight that brought my attention to what I might otherwise have missed. My enthusiasm had already dismissed the $25-over-budget rent as "close enough." I said a silent prayer: *Thank you God, Spirit, Higher Power, whoever it is that is looking after me. I do so appreciate your stepping in and grabbing my attention.*

Following His Own Advice

David was not pleased when I told him the place wouldn't do. He wasn't convinced that the burnt-out lightbulb was a sign urging me to keep looking. "But Ann, this is the only listing in the entire town that might possibly meet your needs, and you're almost out of time." I believed what he said but wouldn't change my mind.

I realized that David was not following his own good advice. Hadn't he been the one who taught me to hold out for what I really wanted? Hadn't he shown me through story and personal example just what was possible when I was willing to affirm and believe? Maybe he had never learned about signs and signals from the Universe. However, I now was placing my faith in them.

Quite frankly, I amazed myself with how confidently I continued to believe that the perfect new home would show up in time. If this house wasn't it, so be it. I simply had to keep looking, living in faith and trust. As the deadline approached, I continued affirming: *Before August 31st of this year, I move into a bright, attractive, wonderfully nurturing, easily affordable, modern home that superbly meets all my needs.*

Getting More Than I Asked For

When David called a few days later, he dampened his enthusiasm as he described another seemingly perfect match that had just come on the market that morning. It had everything on my wish list. When I saw it, I was ecstatic. It had trees, big rooms, lots of light, great office space, two-and-one-half baths, plenty of bedrooms and was in a quiet neighborhood. It was perfect, and, get this, the rent was $50 a month less than my budget – a bargain that couldn't be beat!

I had met my deadline with a few days and a few dollars to spare. As I said, "Yes, yes, yes!" to David, I also said a prayer: "Thank you, Universe, for giving me such a wonderful new home! Thank you for helping me avoid settling for second-best."

Nearly everyone who came to visit commented on the strong sense of calmness they felt when entering the front door. Some even mentioned the house felt healing – and these were friends who knew nothing about energy, metaphysics or similar things. The Universe had truly given me more than I had asked for. It was the perfect environment in which to rest and heal, now that I was out of bed and on my feet.

 **Try This**

- Instead of settling for second-best, consider aiming for the ideal. Trust the Universe to provide exactly what you need and be willing to do your part to make it happen. When you turn down what doesn't suit, you give the Universe the time it needs to create something better and more perfect.

- Pay attention to possible signs and signals from the Universe that symbolically convey messages of confirmation or warning.

- Consider that "bad" news might actually be good news, and be grateful when you find out afterward how you benefited.

- Always remember to thank God, the Universe, Higher Power or whatever you choose to call it, for the gift. The more positive energy you put out, the more it will be returned.

TEN

The Baby Needed Milk
Flowing With Life

Missed Turns

What is coincidence? Is it just a twist of fate, the coming together of miscellaneous factors that somehow fall into place as a fortuitous event? Or could there be a mysterious force driving events?

I once attended an enlightening weekend conference sponsored by the Association for Humanistic Psychology. For the first time in my life, I was surrounded by people who, I was sure, would not scoff at the strange events occurring in my life and how I interpreted them. Our like-mindedness was exhilarating.

Driving home late at night, super tired after a long and fascinating day, I was thinking about all I had learned when I suddenly realized I missed my turn. *Oh well*, I thought. *I'll simply keep going the way I'm headed. It's not worth the trouble to turn around; this other route is only slightly longer.*

Next thing I knew, I had missed the next turn as well. *Oh shucks*, I sighed once again. *I might as well stop by the convenience store for a cup of coffee since it's now on my way. I could obviously use it.*

Only a $100 Bill

As I entered the store, I overheard an upset customer plead, "Please, my baby needs milk. We're totally out." The cashier replied curtly, "I don't have change for a $100 bill."

"But that's all I've got!" the distraught father replied. Back and forth the argument went. The store clerk was not willing to let the man take the milk without paying for it.

Now I knew why I had missed all those turns, taking the extra long way home. "I've got change for a hundred," I interrupted. Fortunately, I had been to the bank earlier that day. It was clear providence had steered me to this store so I could help a father buy milk for his hungry baby.

Winning Without Sacrifice

Both the father and I were winners that night. He got his milk and I got a cup of hot coffee, plus the opportunity to experience the principle of synchronicity in action. It was as if this experience had been created just for me.

Synchronicity is when two or more events take place in some meaningful way, but there is no logical causal connection between them. In other words, "chance" encounters might be more than they appear. True synchronistic events benefit both parties even though this is not always apparent.

Life works best when we go with the flow. When we allow ourselves to momentarily relinquish control, we invite the Universe to guide us. As we adjust to the needs of the moment, allowing a situation to unfold, we're likely to be glad things happened as they did. We may even discover good reasons for "stupid mistakes."

Try This

- Watch for signs and signals. Be open to clues that might suggest alternative interpretations. Assume things are happening for a good reason.

- Take note when synchronistic events occur: A distant friend you've been thinking about calls out of the blue. Pay attention to coincidences: The doctor's office cancels your appointment and you were wondering if it was important to attend a meeting that was scheduled for the same afternoon. The more aware we are that we're being gently supported and guided, the easier it becomes to consciously tune in to receive further messages.

- Think about a current situation that has been frustrating or upsetting. Ask yourself, "Have I been flowing with what wants to happen or trying to take things in the direction I prefer?" If control and resistance are your usual pattern, why not try something different? Use the situation as an opportunity to try on new behavior – that of letting go. Allow the event to unfold as if it has a mind of its own and knows how it wants things to go. Remember, when we let them, "'wrong" turns often turn out to be the best alternative after all.

- Talk about synchronicity and coincidence with people who might be able to solidify your own understanding. Discuss such questions as: When is coincidence just a coincidence – or is there no such thing as an accident? Do synchronicities happen every day or just occasionally? Can we make them happen more frequently? What would it mean if we had such power?

ELEVEN

I Never Saw the Red Light
Trusting Your Experience

Time Stood Still

On the third day of the Humanistic Psychology conference I was attending, I had overslept. Running late, I sped toward campus, relieved to see one of the last traffic lights was green. Quickly hanging a left, I proceeded to zip through.

Halfway through the intersection, as I looked to my right through the passenger window, I saw a frightening sight. I was about to be hit broadside by a rush of oncoming traffic. They were going far too fast to avoid crashing into me full force.

At that very moment, the traffic seemed to stop in mid-motion. It was as if I had pushed the pause button on a movie I was watching. My car was the only one moving. Time stood still. I heard nothing but total silence. Absolute quiet. It was then I realized the light must have been red, though I felt sure I had seen a green arrow.

Before I could contemplate further, the action started up again. Horns honked as the oncoming traffic sped past – inches from the tail end of my car – filling the space where I had just been.

There was no logical explanation for what had just happened. Instead, the incident significantly reinforced that I was on the right track with my three-month experiment. The Universe had grabbed my attention in a more spectacular way than ever before, as if making sure I got the message:

Do you see now, Ann? The world doesn't always operate according to earth-plane rules. We created this experience to help you overcome your doubt. You had trouble believing in mini-miracles, so we decided to give you a big Miracle with a capital "M" – something you couldn't possibly explain away logically.

It was true. Despite what had happened so far, I still struggled with believing I had really dissolved clouds, received messages from butterflies, healed with my hands. But, by escaping what should have been an inescapable disaster, I had been given a gift, a reward for being willing to open my mind to new ways of thinking and being. My near-miss experience had defied the laws of physics – time had literally stood still.

Potent Fumes

Strange events like these were taking place in my life with increasing frequency. I wondered what would happen next.

Overcoming my reluctance to tell anyone what had happened, for fear I'd not be believed, I shared my story with a stranger I had just met. Phoebe was delighted with my "never saw the red light" tale, and told me about her own hard-to-believe experience – which she had long been reluctant to talk about for the very same reasons. Once again, I was rewarded for my commitment to explore and experiment, sticking my neck out, subjecting myself to possible ridicule. Once again, I had been guided to the right person. Here's the story Phoebe shared that day.

After spending several years at Findhorn, Phoebe was now living deep in the Oregon woods. One night, she received a phone call from a friend in crisis. Though it was nearly midnight,

Phoebe felt it imperative to leave immediately; her presence was needed.

She had been driving for about an hour before it dawned on her to check the gas gauge. The tank was nearly empty. Phoebe knew there wasn't a gas station for another 50 miles, and at that hour, it would be closed. She had to make a decision. What should she do?

Faced with a 200-mile journey through a sparsely populated area on an empty tank of gas, Phoebe chose the only alternative she saw available: She said a prayer for Divine intervention and kept on driving. There was no sense turning around since she didn't have enough gas to get back home, and her friend really needed her.

Five hours later, Phoebe arrived at her destination with the gas gauge still on empty. It seemed for most of the trip her car had been powered by some mighty potent fumes.

It Helps to Share

One extraordinary tale tends to trigger others. These outlandish incidents prompted a memory of when I was about 10 years old and heard the Universe sing. Not having anyone to tell who wouldn't doubt or scoff, I never said a word, and soon forgot the incident. I had not thought about it for decades, and it never happened again.

I've learned it's human nature to dismiss and forget what doesn't fit our understanding of how the world works. Without the reminding and reinforcement that comes from sharing our stories, these memories tend to blur and bury themselves so deep, they don't resurface until something significant leads to possibly remembering.

Have you ever experienced something so strange that you never told anyone for fear they'd laugh or disbelieve? By sharing my traffic light story with Phoebe, I gained the confidence to believe what I had experienced really had happened. Time really had been suspended long enough to save my life.

Try This

- If something out of the ordinary should occur, allow yourself to believe your experience. Too often we dismiss what doesn't make sense so we don't have to think about what we can't explain. It helps to share and write it down.

- Think back over the past and see if you can recall any unusual incidents that didn't make logical sense. Don't expect to remember; you might or might not. Maybe nothing strange has ever happened. The point is simply to consider the possibility.

- Share your stories (or share my story) with friends, or maybe a stranger, for then it doesn't matter if they judge you crazy or foolish, you'll never see them again. Ask people if they've ever heard of, or experienced their own, inexplicable events. It could lead to interesting conversation, and you might discover more people who are also curious about miraculous occurrences and your own experiments.

TWELVE

I'd Been Doing It All Along
Healing Hands

A Charlatan for Sure

It is common knowledge that our circulatory and nervous systems are key connective components of the physical body. What is not well known, however, is that energy also permeates and surrounds our physical being and is equally important to healing and good health.

If it had not been for my commitment to try on anything that was new and different, part of my *Experiments in Living*™, I never would have become friends with Barbara. She was into some mighty weird ideas as far as I was concerned. Barbara suggested I attend an upcoming Reiki workshop to explore what I knew nothing about.

Reiki is one of many methods for channeling energy, or *chi*, to promote healing and health. The technique uses the hands, palms and fingers to deliver *chi* to specified parts of the body. It helps remove blockages and otherwise facilitate the normal free flow of our vital life force.

At the Reiki workshop, the facilitators told us that when we transmit energy, it is often felt as heat or cold or tingling in the palms of our hands. Several hours into the first class, half the students claimed, "I can feel it, I can feel it!" But I couldn't feel a thing; not a single sensation. For want of a better explanation, I assumed I had witnessed my first case of group hypnosis.

At the end of the day, we were led through an initiation ceremony. As we sat in a circle surrounded by candles and soft music, the workshop leader wrapped me on the head with his knuckles and mumbled some kind of incantation. My suspicions were confirmed: He was a fraud and a charlatan.

Curing Headaches

That evening, I went to a picnic with a new friend, Al, who seemed quite knowledgeable about spiritual and metaphysical concepts. Shortly after we arrived, his teenage son announced, "Dad, I've got a headache." Al laid his hand on his son's forehead. A minute later his son said, "Thanks Dad, it's gone now."

What's going on here? I thought. *Does this have anything to do with the Reiki workshop I just attended?* I had dismissed the class as a lot of nonsense, but no one else in our conversational circle at the picnic indicated surprise at Al's healing ability. Everyone seemed to accept this unusual cure for headaches as normal and natural. Having just seen evidence that people can heal with their hands, I was forced to reconsider my opinion of Reiki.

The Gift of Healing

As I observed Al bring relief to his son, I recalled some of my own successes in curing peoples' headaches. Maybe there was a connection between Reiki and the head massages for headaches I had been giving for years. To my string of successes, I decided to find out if I could apply my skills to other parts of the body.

My first experiment involved a man I had just been introduced to. As we shook hands in greeting, Dan apologized for his cold and clammy hands. He said they had been that way for years. Rarely could he get them warm, and yes, it was quite uncomfortable.

Hesitantly, I told Dan that I had recently discovered I might have the gift of healing. Would he like me to try healing his hands? "Sure, why not? I've got nothing to lose," he replied.

I put Dan's right hand between mine and concentrated on sending white light and healing energy. Within a minute, Dan exclaimed, "You won't believe what's happening. My other hand is warming up, too." When I reached over to touch his free hand, I was astonished at the difference. It was toasty warm.

Courage to Continue

Experiences like this gave me the courage to continue experimenting. I was still quite concerned about what people would think, recalling how harshly I had judged the Reiki workshop leader, who probably wasn't a fraud after all.

As the months went by, I was motivated to learn more about how healing hands worked. Every time I shifted imagery or hand position on my "patients," I would ask them to describe their experience. I used their feedback, and my intuition, to teach myself hands-on healing. Over time, my technique improved. Since then this gift has been tested and proved time and again.

Anything Was Worth a Try

One of my favorite healing stories is about the time my daughter fell, and we thought she might have broken a rib. As we waited in the emergency room for the doctor to examine her, a baby wailed loudly in the curtained cubicle next to ours. My daughter suggested that I see if I could help. "If you really do have the gift of healing," she said, "now would be the time to use it."

I introduced myself to the child's grandmother and offered to try my hand at healing. I gave her my now standard disclaimer: "I can't promise it will work, but I can guarantee it will do no harm. I don't even have to touch the baby." His temperature was 105° F; nothing they had tried so far could bring it down. Anything was worth a try, the grandmother said.

Within minutes, the baby had stopped crying. As he reached out for me to hold him, his grandmother expressed great surprise, "He never goes to strangers. He always gets upset and pulls away when anyone but family is near." When the nurse came in to take the baby's temperature, it had dropped to 102° F.

A Thousand Pin Pricks

I returned to my daughter's side to find her in a lot of pain. "Why don't you try some of your healing on me?" she asked. "I sure could use it." So I did – and I got the surprise of my life.

My hands started tingling, as if a thousand pins prickled my palms. As I passed my hands over the length of her body, the tingling changed from extreme to none at all. Wherever she hurt, I could feel it.

For the first time, I could feel the energy flowing, just like the people in the Reiki workshop. Ever since then, I've felt a small degree of sensitivity, which helps guide my hands to where healing energy is needed.

Developing Your Skills

As I tried my skills on friends and acquaintances, I would ask them to let me know if anything significant occurred. I seldom heard a word, even from those who had been immediately cured of a long-standing, painful problem. It's no wonder it took a whole lot for me to gain confidence that I really did have the gift of healing with my hands.

It took me quite a while to figure out why I wasn't getting the feedback I requested. I discovered it's difficult for people to acknowledge what they don't understand and never thought possible. It's human nature to downplay and deny what might make them appear foolish in the eyes of the rest of the world.

As my skill and understanding grew, I noticed that when I was tired, discouraged or not feeling good about myself, my healing powers diminished or disappeared all together. When I had lots of energy, and was able to set aside my own personal concerns, my abilities returned and were stronger.

It's most important, however, that I not take credit for whatever healing happens. I am not the cause, only the conduit. It's not me doing the healing; I'm only providing the hands that channel the energy, directing heat and light to where it's needed.

I also learned that you don't need to understand how or why the process works in order for it to work. I had been using my healing gifts long before I had even heard about Reiki and laying-on-of-hands healing.

Try This

- To find out if you also have healing hands, ask your "patients" what part of their body needs attention. Have them describe the pain or discomfort and its probable cause. Rub your hands together rapidly to create enough friction to generate a wee bit of warmth. This gets the energy flowing.

- Focus your attention on your "patient" and what you are doing. Don't talk, just see if you can feel or sense anything. Once you've developed your skills, you can be effective while carrying on a conversation.

- Imagine energy or white light entering the top of your head. Send it down your arms and out through the palms of your hands and the ends of your fingers to the area of discomfort.

- While some healers touch the body, I prefer to hold my hands 1 to 3 inches above the area I'm concentrating upon. This enables me to be more aware of sensations; I'm not distracted by the feel of cloth or skin.

- Notice any sensations in your hands. It may take a few minutes, or it may not happen at all. Realize that lack of sensation does not mean lack of healing.

- Begin by scanning the body, very slowly. See what you notice. You may feel something in an area seemingly unrelated to where the problem is reported. Sometimes this heals the problem; sometimes people need extra energy focused on a number of different spots in the body.

- Ask your "patient" for feedback, to report what she notices. Move your hands around, let the heat and tingling in your hands guide you, and listen to your intuition. If your "patient" doesn't report any sensations, try repositioning your hands slightly, or move them to another part of the body. After a few minutes, ask again if she notices anything.

- Remember, people who are unfamiliar with energy healing may withhold pertinent information. Do not let this discourage you. Ask questions and make your "patients" feel as comfortable as possible about the experience. Encourage them to explore the unknown and unfamiliar.

- If you find that you have an innate gift to heal, consider taking a course in Reiki, Polarity Therapy or any other form of hands-on healing. You needn't take a course to get started, but professional training will help you develop your skills far more rapidly than you could on your own.

THIRTEEN

A Field Full of Feathers
Overcoming Fear and Doubt

Fear of Losing

Having known Al for just a short time, I felt apprehensive as I told him about my experiences dissolving clouds. I described how I'd had a series of successes, then became scared I wouldn't be able to do it again and finally stopped experimenting altogether.

"Oh that!" he replied. "Every time I go flying, I imagine clear skies overhead." It was his next comment that really caught my attention. "Fear of losing what you have will stop you every time."

He was right. I had been afraid of losing my growing belief in the Power of Belief. I was afraid to fail because that would prove the Power of Belief didn't work.

Skies All Clear

Al continued with a story about an airport manager who gave him a funny look one day as Al drove into the parking lot. "I don't get it Al," the airport manager said, shaking his head. "It was cloudy when you called this morning. Now it's clear. I've been noticing that whenever you show up, the clouds disappear and everyone gets to fly. I just don't get it."

Without another word, Al reported, the manager headed toward the hangar mumbling to himself, not even curious enough to ask a single question, to wonder further, to hear what Al might have to say about it.

I was curious, however, and thought I knew what Al's explanation would be. "Act as if, huh?" I queried. "Yes, Ann, it's as simple as that. As I leave the house, I imagine clear skies overhead. That's why I always get to fly, even on cloudy days."

Al then added the most important lesson of all: "All that's required is desire, belief and acceptance."

Desire Required

Al explained, "Nothing can happen unless we really want it to. Without desire, there's no reason to take action or to follow through. Our desire needs to be strong enough to make us willing to do what it takes to overcome resistance to exploring different possibilities and discovering new truths. It's human nature to resist the unknown, what's unfamiliar. It's easier, more comfortable, to hang out in the way things have always been."

Belief in What?

The desire part I got. I really wanted those clouds to disappear, to prove it was possible. It was the believing part that made me shaky. "Belief in what?" I inquired. "I don't understand what I'm supposed to believe in."

"It doesn't matter, Ann," Al continued. "You don't have to define it. Just believe that whatever you want to occur, will. That's all there is to it."

"Act as if, huh?" I once again queried for confirmation.

"Yes, just continue acting as if these mini-miracles were normal," Al said. "Explanations will eventually reveal themselves. If you try to understand something before you've actually experienced it, preconceived notions will distort your observations.

Total Acceptance

Al had reminded me of what I had already learned. Doubt and disbelief make us overlook, discount or explain away what is undeniable. The more willing we are to suspend all doubt, the more we empower ourselves. When we let go of resistance, we are better able to let things happen, help them happen, see and acknowledge the evidence that proves they did.

Al continued. "If we expect specific results or positive proof with every affirmation or request, we set ourselves up for failure and disappointment. Whatever happens, assume it happens for a good reason – which we may or may not discover later."

I thought about David and Joan's house-buying plans falling through, since they were divorced soon after. Al kept speaking, "We need to be willing to accept the unexpected, even if it seems a disappointment at first. Guaranteed, everything that happens holds the seed of something good."

Zeroed In

"You still don't realize, *you* have the power to make things happen," Al emphasized. "Probably one of the main reasons you're having trouble accepting this truth is that you don't yet realize everyone has this ability. You're not unique. You're just like everyone else."

I sighed with relief. This time Al had zeroed in on what was really bothering me. I was afraid of this new-found power. The state of the world makes clear what awfulness happens when too many people abuse and misuse power. I most certainly did not want to be like that. Having put the finger on what was bothering me freed me to realize that Al was talking about a different kind of power.

Tangible Proof

Snapping his fingers, eyes sparkling in anticipation, Al declared, "I've got an idea! What you need now is some sort of tangible proof that you have the power to create the future you choose. That everyone has the power to manifest what they want." Sounded like a good idea to me.

"Everything you've experienced so far can be attributed to something else. The wind blew the clouds away; your mother would have sent money anyway; your near miss in the car was just your imagination. It didn't happen," he said. Al had my attention.

"Have you read Richard Bach's book *Illusions*? The main character is a reluctant messiah who decides to practice his newly discovered creative powers by making a blue feather appear. Guess where it showed up? On a milk carton. That's where he found a picture of a blue feather. You have to be open, Ann, to letting the Universe provide in unexpected ways."

Al then asked me a couple of pointed questions: "If you declare your intention to find a blue feather, or any other item you choose, and it shows up, will you accept that as proof that you made it happen? Will you allow yourself to believe that it was your willingness to believe that created tangible proof?"

"OK, I'll do it!" I declared with a conviction that I wasn't sure I could uphold. I didn't tell Al that I would have been happy to receive *any* color feather the Universe wanted to deliver! Deep down, I was still afraid of losing my new belief in the Power of Belief, so I didn't want to make this first test too difficult.

Aglow With Anticipation

As I shifted into "act-as-if" mode, setting my fears aside, I felt aglow with excitement and anticipation. No more doubts. No more questions. I just "knew" it would happen.

I began imagining how wonderful it would feel to finally have tangible proof that the Power of Belief really worked. Wanting to express my heart-felt gratitude to Al for showing me the way, I decided to give him the most precious gift I could. The feather I would find. A symbol of the Power of Belief to create desired results.

Thoughts of my three daughters popped into my head, followed by thoughts of dear friends, people with whom I most wanted to share my good news. After telling my story, I would give each a feather so they, too, could have a physical reminder of the Power of Belief. Maybe it would encourage them to try their own experiments and explore these questions further.

Suddenly, my thoughts were interrupted by a big dose of reality: *I can't attract 12 feathers! It's just not possible. I don't live where birds tend to congregate. Finding one feather is going to be hard enough!*

I Hedged My Bet

But then I realized I would be denying my friends and family a truly precious gift. Tangible evidence that what we think and believe really does have the power to create intended results. What I most wanted was to share my good news with the most important people in my life. I was going to have to find enough feathers for everyone if I was to be able to give them their own reminding symbol of what's truly possible.

If I was going to aim for the impossible, it would be wise to give it an extra few days. Besides, it seemed inconsiderate to ask on such short notice for something so difficult. I was requesting a lot more than just a single feather. So I gave myself five days to find a dozen – any color, motley brown would do.

A Startling Sight

Fortunately, I was still attending the week-long Humanistic Psychology conference at American University. Every hour or so, we walked across campus to another talk, which gave me frequent opportunities to look for feathers. I did it every chance I got.

I had no luck the first day. Nor the second. No matter how hard I looked, the third day came up empty handed as well. Not one single feather showed up.

On my way to lunch the fourth day of affirming my intention to find a dozen feathers, I came across a sight that startled me into stopping and staring. Scattered over a huge lawn was a sea of feathers. It was as if there had been a huge pillow fight up in the sky and this was the result.

I swooped down on that field full of feathers and began scooping up as many as I could, stuffing them into my pockets and purse. I sent profuse thanks to the Universe for such a marvelous response to my request.

Tears of Gratitude

Sticking a feather in my name tag – to remind me of the Power of Belief that had just been so profoundly proved – I headed off to lunch. The woman ahead of me in line turned to chat, beginning the conversation with a question.

"Why are you wearing a feather in your name tag?" she asked. I asked if she wanted to hear the short or long version. "The long version, definitely," she said.

So I told her about creating parking places, healing headaches and dissolving clouds. I shared how I got scared that I couldn't do it anymore, and what Al had said about desire, belief and acceptance, and how important it is to let go of the need for proof.

As I described finding the field full of feathers, tears rolled down the woman's face. "I can't thank you enough!" she cried. "What can I do for you in return?"

I was totally taken aback. I had no idea what she was talking about. I hadn't done anything but tell her a story and show her all the feathers I had found.

The Long Version

Realizing the profound affect my Feather Story had on this woman, I gave her a feather. She said she would treasure it forever and put it in her name tag as I had done.

As the conference continued, more people asked about the feather in my name tag. Soon, it became obvious that an inordinate number of people were inquiring – more than you'd expect. I was even more surprised when every single person said they wanted the long version of the story. I was truly astounded when every listener reacted as strongly as the woman in the lunch line. I got an unbelievable number of hugs and heartfelt thanks that day.

All told, I repeated the story about a dozen times. Everyone made it clear how important my Feather Story had been for them. Now I knew why I had collected far more than the dozen feathers I needed for family and friends!

Try This

- Pass this book on to people who might be receptive. It could trigger some very interesting discussions. Ask people what they believe, if they believe in the Power of Belief, if they know how to manifest and create everyday miracles.

- Share your own Feather Stories with those who are interested. Talk about the experiments you've conducted and what happens as a result. Let go of worrying about how others might judge you; choose to be of service instead.

- Share your story with me. Tell me what happens, I'd love to hear. And if I collect enough stories, I'll publish them in a second book. I find stories like these wonderfully reinforcing.

FOURTEEN

Lesson Learned
Waiting Until the Appropriate Moment

What Do You Believe?

A few months after finding my feathers, I spent the afternoon with a new acquaintance. We had a wonderful time discovering how many interests we shared in common. After several hours of such exhilarating conversation, we were both tired, our brains were drained, we needed a break. Just as I was about to say 'good-bye, I look forward to getting together again,' Bob asked a question totally unrelated to anything we'd been discussing. "What do you believe in, Ann? Are you on the Spiritual Path?

It turned out Bob felt like something was missing from his life. He'd clearly been pondering the question for quite some time, not at all sure what he believed, or how to figure it out.

I took Bob through the same long version you now know about parking places and healing hands, dissolving clouds and getting scared, and finally finding more than a dozen feathers. I left Bob with the suggestion that he, too, try to find a feather (or whatever else he might choose), asking him to let me know if anything happened.

Wonderful Whopper

Bob never called, so I assumed it hadn't worked. Several weeks later, I called him about another matter. As we were about to hang up, I casually inquired, "By the way, did you try to find a feather?"

"Ah ... er ...," he stammered. Obviously, Bob didn't want to talk about it. Nevertheless, he hesitantly began sharing the results of his experiment. Here's the whopper of a tale he told.

Bob had decided to find a feather, as I had done – and the reluctant messiah of Richard Bach's *Illusions*. Bob actually found a feather the very next day in the toe of his fishing boot. How it got there he had no idea. He was adamant the boots had been thoroughly washed at the end of the season the previous year. This was standard procedure, for who wanted a hall closet smelling all winter of dead fish?

"But it really didn't mean anything," he stammered and insisted.

"Of course not," I assured. "As I told you, don't worry about proof or what you believe. All you need do at this point is to acknowledge what happens. In time, your questions will answer themselves. For right now, focus on exploring possibilities and gathering information. You can decide what to believe later."

But this wasn't the end of his story. Bob unhappily continued. "A few hours later, my wife yelled, 'Come quick. You won't believe what I just found!' It turned out, while cleaning the storage closet, right there in a box she had taped up several years previously, were oodles of feathers. She kept wondering where they had come from, how they could have possibly gotten there. I told her I didn't know."

"You mean you hadn't told her what we talked about?" I asked in surprise. He hadn't. And it was obvious that he wasn't going to let her in on his little secret, that maybe he just might have had something to do with the feathers showing up.

As Bob told me this second story, I could hear the consternation in his voice. He really didn't want to be telling me what had happened. He kept assuring me it wasn't evidence of anything significant.

I, of course, considered it a powerful example of what we can do when we're willing to say what we want and believe it will happen. *Yea, yea!* I silently said to myself. *Sounds as though you need a herd of trumpeting elephants to rain down on your head, to get you to admit something significant took place!* I wanted to tell Bob but didn't.

Out loud I restated my reassurances that he didn't have to accept finding those extra feathers as proof of anything. All I asked, for his sake, was that he simply take notice and acknowledge what had happened. It wasn't necessary to draw conclusions, to believe anything in particular.

His story didn't end here, either.

Bob tried to convince me that the next incident was nothing more than pure coincidence. "Just because it happened on the very same day as the previous two episodes...," Bob began, using absurdly convoluted logic to attempt to explain away what happened next.

Later that same afternoon, Bob had begun preparing his van for an upcoming camping trip. As he opened the side doors, an overflowing abundance of feathers flew about, scattering everywhere.

"Somehow a bird must have gotten inside the van and gone berserk," he said. "I never found the bird nor what might have caused the mayhem."

As Bob hemmed and hawed his way through this surprise ending to an already impressive sequence of events, he continued to do his level best to keep affirming that nothing extraordinary had occurred.

Bob had two choices: He could either deny or believe that he might have had something to do with all those feathers repeatedly popping up in some mighty unlikely places. It didn't matter to me. I already knew what was true. Even spread out over several months, the bizarre nature of those three incidents would have been more than enough to persuade the average person.

But Bob was the one who wanted to find belief. Evidently – obviously – he wasn't ready to have his prayers answered. He wasn't ready to believe the proof being so generously provided. He was in denial. He wanted to forget.

Pause to Consider

Hindsight often teaches us the lessons we need to know. Bob's inability to accept three major mini-miracles in a single day showed me how important it is not to let our enthusiasm run away with us. If we push our stories on people who aren't ready, if we rush to share when the timing's not right, if we present our ideas too quickly, we strengthen their resistance to the challenging new ideas we present.

Before Bob asked if I was on the spiritual path, we were already worn out from a long afternoon of stimulating conversation. It wasn't the time to begin a brand new topic. What would have happened if I had paused to consider: *Is now the best time to tell Bob my Feather Stories*?

I also knew all was not for naught. While Bob wasn't ready to accept what had happened, the principles of my Feather Stories were now lodged in his subconscious, available to be reflected upon when the time was right.

Try This

- As you share your stories and experiences, ask yourself: Is now a good time for this person to hear what I have to say, or would it be better to wait? Is this person likely to be open-minded to hearing and learning about the Power of Belief?

- Ask your listeners if they want to hear the short or long version of your story. If they want the summary version, your purpose will simply be to plant a few seeds. It's important not to overwhelm people with ideas they are not yet ready to consider.

- Accept that people may not believe you, or even be interested. They might consider you crazy, naïve or stupid. Or they could be deeply grateful. Your job is to tell a story so people can draw their own conclusions, as I have done with you.

- Have fun playing the Feather Finding game. Belief is stronger when it's reinforced with results. Try asking to find a $10 bill, a brown shoe lace, a red dress, whatever you choose.

- If you find these Feather Stories upsetting – if you don't feel ready, if you're super tired, under a lot of stress – set aside thinking about it for a while. Take a break. The information isn't going away. It's in your memory bank now. It's in this book you are reading, available to be re-read when the time is right for deeper consideration.

FIFTEEN

What Am I to Believe
One, Two, Three

The Big Question

That's my Feather Story – the long version. Isn't it a beaut?! I hope it serves you well. The living of it certainly turned my life around.

What is the source of this power? What is the Creative Force that co-operates and co-creates with us when we send a prayer or speak an affirmation? This is the question I've delayed answering until you had sufficient personal experience to be able to understand my answers; there are several.

ONE – It Doesn't Matter

It doesn't matter whether you believe it's God or the Man in the Moon who causes things to happen. You can call it Life, Holy Spirit, the Universe … Self, Source, Creator of All That Is … however you name it or describe it, it does not change what happens. Your belief is all that's needed to manifest what you choose.

TWO – YOU have the Power

You have the power to create what you want. You have the power to make miracles happen as everyday events. Lack of belief, lack of awareness, does not alter this basic Truth.

You activate this power by believing you have it. It is enough to "act as if" you truly believe you have the power to create, to activate the creative powers you seek.

You activate this power by wanting to discover if it really exists, and how you can make it work for you. You learn how to harness your Creative Powers by conducting experiments and talking with fellow explorers. You claim your power by thinking and speaking as positively as possible.

THREE – It's a Mystery

What is it that responds to our prayers and positive affirmations? What is it that stops traffic in mid-air or flows through healing hands?

It's a big, capital M, Mystery. Though saints and sages, poets and shamans have tried for thousands of years to put the Mystery into words, no one has been able to describe it completely. It is beyond human understanding.

Some find their answers in religion. Ever increasing numbers are turning to metaphysics and spirituality as a source of guidance and insight. Metaphysics is the branch of philosophy concerned with the Universal Laws that govern all Life. Spirituality focuses on beliefs held in common by all religions, moving beyond doctrine and dogma.

Experience demonstrates, the more we apply metaphysical and spiritual principles to daily living, the easier it becomes to create what we want in life. What I find exciting is that science has at last begun to understand and confirm what metaphysicians and spiritual sages have been saying for thousands of years.

Whatever you believe, whether it is based on science or religion or a comic book, nothing changes the fact that YOU have the Power of Creation at your fingertips.

The Question is...

- What do *You* believe? Now that you've read my Feather Stories and conducted your own experiments, what have you concluded? Has your own direct experience caused you to alter or question your thinking?

- How does it feel to know you have the power to make miracles happen – mini and major – as everyday events? As my own story illustrates, it's difficult to claim and exercise a power we're afraid of, or don't believe we deserve.

- And a final question: What do you plan to do now? – next? If you want a place to start, I've described numerous resources in the appendices that were especially valuable to me, and Section V will outline some Next Steps suggestions.

Section Three

UNIVERSAL PRINCIPLES

How the Universe Works

New learning is most effective when we review and reinforce what's unfamiliar. The best way to integrate new knowledge is to hear it stated a number of different ways. This section will help you do that. It summarizes the Universal Principles illustrated by the series of Feather Stories. I consider it an essential part of the book.

TRUTH

Truth does not depend on proof. It just is. Truth is Truth. It cannot be altered by a differing opinion.

What we believe determines what we see. Expectations dictate what we experience, conclude and create.

An open mind is essential to discovering new truths. Until we stop insisting that we know what's true, we view things from a perspective that is limited and biased.

Truth is not always easy to accept. It is human nature to run away from or deny new ideas that are disturbing.

Truth sets us free. When you flow with truth, you live in harmony with what is – how things are right now. Acceptance brings peace and a greater ability to deal with reality.

ENERGY

Everything is energy. Energy is everywhere. Our bodies, rocks and stars are different forms of energy. Only the densities and speeds of vibration differ.

Thought is energy. Thought energized with emotion is even more powerful. Loving thought is a nurturing force that can cause plants to blossom beyond the norm. Children and animals are especially sensitive and responsive.

Energy can be channeled for healing. Some people have a special talent for channeling a laser-like force of healing light through their hands.

We are the channel for, not the source of, healing energy. We cannot rightfully take credit for the cures we produce. We do not manufacture the healing energy, we only funnel and focus the healing Light of Spirit.

THOUGHT

The mind is not as smart as we think. Our minds are pattern seekers. Once a thought structure is built, the mind ignores what seems extraneous or irrelevant. Only by choosing to scan for missed variables, to pay attention to blips of new information, can we challenge old beliefs and build more accurate ways of thinking.

Thought creates reality. The mind has the power to create and destroy, whether it be parking places or dissolving clouds. Therefore, it is imperative to examine our beliefs and convictions if we are to create the kind of life we want.

We choose what we think. Thoughts pop into our heads at random. We choose whether to pursue or ignore, to agree or disagree. We choose whether to hang on to old, erroneous beliefs collected since childhood or to challenge their validity and replace them with what better serves us.

We can reprogram our thoughts. Affirmations are valuable tools for changing harmful thinking patterns into helpful ones. It's important to do them correctly to avoid undermining good intentions. Make them short and succinct. Use positive language and adjectives that trigger enlivening images.

ATTITUDE

Life supports those who help themselves. It's not enough to pray and wish for things. We must be willing to let go of what keeps us from experiencing the benevolent abundance of the Universe.

Every negative holds the seed of an equally powerful positive. Positive and negative are two sides of the same coin. They are interpretations we place upon a neutral event. We choose how we view each situation.

Life works best when we flow with what's happening. By trying to maintain control, we cut off Higher Power assistance. How can we know we have found a better way unless we're willing to try another way? Assume whatever your situation that it is happening for a reason. Could it be a good reason?

LEARNING

When the student is ready, the teacher appears. The fact that these pages somehow found their way into your hands is one possible example of how the Universe provides and guides. As Bob's inability to acknowledge the significance of all those feathers demonstrates, we don't have to accept what is freely offered.

Experience is the best teacher. The only way to know something for sure is to give it an open-minded try. The more we explore new thoughts and new ways of doing things – the more we experiment with how we live our lives – the greater the likelihood we'll uncover a number of life-altering Truths we might have otherwise missed.

If you want to learn, pay attention. We cannot be influenced by the things we choose to ignore. Notice what's new or different. Look for patterns. Gather evidence. Question appearances. Try assuming there's more going on than you think.

Don't expect specific results. Expectation limits our senses and stifles awareness, causing us to overlook other possibilities. And, expectation creates disappointment. When we are open to whatever happens, we're far more likely to be happy with what we get.

Trust your intuition. Recognize you can intuitively "know" what your mind cannot figure out. Anyone can learn to use this amazingly accurate source of information, all it takes is practice.

ANSWERS

The most powerful answers are the ones we discover for ourselves. Otherwise we're trusting someone else's opinion, and I don't know any two people who agree 100 percent about everything. Do you?

Answers and assistance show up when we're ready. Patience is usually required. Have you told the Universe what you want?

The Universe communicates through signs and signals. We choose the methods that speak to us most clearly. Mechanical things (this includes electronics) and body symptoms are common communication systems. Play with interpretations, look for patterns, and in time you will teach yourself what you need to know.

Don't expect everyone to agree with you. This will never happen. Share your discoveries with people whose opinions you respect.

CREATING

Desire is the first step to creating. Desire stimulates awareness and action. It makes us more likely to see what's already available, to notice things we might otherwise have missed, to clarify what needs doing to get what we want.

You'll see it when you believe it and not before. If you don't think something is possible, if you don't believe you deserve to have what you want, all the desiring in the world can't make it happen.

If you're not sure you believe, "act as if" you do. If we test reality intellectually from the outside, we'll keep coming up with the same old answers. Only by trying on a new thought system or way of seeing things can we learn if it is valid and really works.

Acceptance and trust is a must. Remember, whatever unpleasantness occurs, it could be just what you need to move you toward your goal. We often don't realize how many in-between steps there are before we get what we want. Every process takes as long as it takes to unfold.

BOTTOM-LINE MESSAGE

- What we do or don't believe determines what we see, experience, conclude and achieve.

- We cannot find Truth unless we are willing to change our minds.

- The more we are guided by how the world really works, rather than what we prefer to believe, the happier and more effective we can be.

- Everyone is a potential Miracle-Maker.

- We all have the power to create the future we choose.

- Miracles become everyday events for those willing to believe and learn.

Section Four

TITHING EXPERIMENT

Preface Revisited

It was suggested in the Preface that you declare the value you intended to receive from *Miracles Made Easy*. Now it's time to adjust that figure up or down.

Did the book fulfill its promise to teach you how to create miracles? Did it reinforce and expand upon what you already knew? How glad are you that you read this book?

What monetary value do you now place on what you've learned and gained? Once again I suggest you write that figure down here $_____ or next to your original book mark amount.

Now Is the Time

The Preface was not part of the original book. I'd finished writing, and my editor was nearly done her part, when an Inner Prompting suggested I add another section, on a brand new topic. I was being shown how people could expand their miracle making powers. A way to get people started on the next step.

Money is a major issue for most people. Now we'd focus people's miracle making powers on their personal finances. It would make an ideal "Experiment in Living"™ to conduct. I already had the center piece for this section written.

A dozen years ago, out of the blue, this same Voice for Spirit requested that I write about Tithing – a subject I knew nothing about and wasn't particularly interested in. I'm so very glad I did. Over time, as I integrated new ways of thinking and being, radical improvements in my life became obviously evident. Decades of living fearfully close to the financial edge were converted into a growing experience of ever-increasing abundance in all areas of my life.

Just as *Miracles Made Easy* languished in a file drawer for ages, *Tithing – A Way of Life* has long awaited Spirit's call to action. I was now being urged to put these two long-in-development writings together, for they were clearly related and would be mutually supportive. Tithing was a logical next step to introduce at this time.

Why Tithe

Here are five good reasons to tithe:

1. It feels good.

2. Some form of *thank you* is always appropriate when someone contributes to our welfare and well being.

3. Expressing gratitude is essential to the creation process. If we don't tell the Universe how happy we are for what we've already received, we have not communicated our desire for more of the same.

4. The more we tithe to those who contribute to the welfare and well being of others, the more we increase their capacity to contribute still further. The greater the numbers tithing to worthy causes, the faster we grow our combined capacity to create a better world.

5. You, too, deserve to be supported and thanked for your own contributions. As they say, *Do unto others as you would have them do unto you.*

Key Points

Keep these key points in mind as you consider whether to conduct another "Experiment in Living"™ - this one focused on tithing and abundance.

1. Tithing is an expression of gratitude for gifts received. Tithes are not confined to money. There are numerous ways to express appreciation and be supportive of those who have contributed to us and the world in which we live.

2. Tithing triggers what is a reciprocal relationship between giving and receiving. The more you give the more you receive. It's Universal Law.

3. Just as you don't need to understand how the Power of Belief and the Power of Thought works in order to create miracles, you don't need to be able to explain how Tithing works to experience its benefits. You just need to do it.

4. "Acting as if" tithing works ... that it really will generate greater abundance ... is the fastest way to integrate this new way of thinking and being.

Now would be a good time to read the short, succinct pamphlet Spirit asked me to write. It's in the Index. One reader said *Tithing – A Way of Life* shifted her from feeling obligated and guilty, to feeling inspired and desiring.

Experiment Explained

As you'll recall, my aim is to make valuable, essential information readily available to all who want it. This means foregoing making a profit and paying expenses out of pocket

A few pages ago I asked if *Miracles Made Easy* had a major or minor impact on you. If you were glad you read it. I am now asking all who answered yes if you will consider Tithing to the author for value received – in whatever way works for you.

While this may seem a self-serving question ... and there's no doubt I will benefit ... its real purpose is to provide an opportunity and stimulus to start you thinking about Tithing – how you feel about sharing what you have, whether you want to reward and support people for gifts received.

Quite frankly, I have no idea what kind of response to expect. What do you think will happen? Will I be reimbursed for expenses incurred? Will there be extra to share with those who so generously contributed their skills to this project? Will I be showered with sufficient funds to finance a next adventure? What do you feel called to do?

If the response is significant enough to be worth reporting, I'll do so at the *Miracles Made Easy* website.

Whatever Happens, I've Been Blessed

As any good experimenter knows, it's essential to keep an open mind, ready to accept whatever results do or don't occur. Whatever happens with this latest "Experiment in Living"™ I am conducting, I feel blessed, for I have already received numerous gifts from writing this book. I love to write, and there's great joy in sharing what has had a profound impact on my well being. I've experienced being supported by many wonderful people, and acquired a number of useful new skills.

The best gift of all has been to be repeatedly reminded with each rewriting that I have the power to create. That miracles can be made to happen with amazing frequency and effortless ease. This is something I don't ever want to forget! *Ever again.*

I will feel doubly – quadruply blessed to learn you have discovered, and claimed, your own creative powers. That you are making miracles happen with ever more confident ease. That you are experiencing the miraculous results of what happens when tithing becomes an ever more natural way of being.

Section Five

NEXT STEPS

Share Your Stories

How can you keep the process going? What will keep you growing and learning? How might you share what's happening with those most likely to be interested? Here are a few suggestions and options.

- Share your own Feather Stories, the results of your own experiments, or share what happened to me with friends and family. Let others benefit as well from what you found most interesting and valuable.

- Share a particular Feather Story with a wider audience, beginning with me. I'd love to hear. If enough people write in, I'll publish them in a follow-up book. You get to see your name in print.

- If you're still plagued by the doubts and disbeliefs that confound so many of us, share your stories and questions with people already familiar with what you are talking about. If you don't know anyone like that right now, simply affirm your intention to attract perfect teachers – people who can guide you like Cynthia, David and Al.

- Pin a feather or any other symbol you choose on your shirt. Wear it for a week or longer. Affirm that it will attract the attention of people who really want whatever stories you choose to share – mine or your own. If you like this idea, select a symbol you can pass out to lots of people – like my feathers – so they'll have a tangible remembrance of the message you shared.

Continue Exploring

When we find a subject useful or interesting, naturally we want to learn more. The question then becomes, where and how? Here are some useful suggestions.

- Check out my list of highly recommended books, spiritual teachers and service providers located in the Appendices.

- Watch the DVD *The Secret*, an introduction to the Law of Attraction, using money and material abundance as the primary example of how the law works. If you can get a copy of the original tape with Abraham/Hicks, that would be better.

- Consider visiting a metaphysical church. Watch Abraham-Hicks on www.YouTube.com.

- Ask questions, of yourself and others. Look through the list of Service Providers in the Appendix for recommendations. If you want to contact me, you'll find that information on the last page of this book.

APPENDICES

Appendix A
Tithing – A Way of Life

Tithing is a spiritual principle to which many aspire, few achieve and hardly anyone fully understands. While many know it to mean the giving of 10% of one's annual income to a church or charity, few are aware of the deeper implications of such donations.

> ***To tithe is to share our resources in a way that expresses heart-felt gratitude to those who have contributed their gifts for our benefit and pleasure, be it personally or by serving the world.***

In other words, the more we benefit, the more those who contribute to us deserve to be comparably rewarded. If we support those who serve us, they are better able to continue serving us and the world still further. By funding good works, tithing becomes a powerfully effective process for co-creating a better world.

Tithing is more than just a feel-good idea. The reasons to tithe, the personal benefits of tithing, are based on current scientific knowledge, as well as religious teachings and ancient philosophical insights.

Metaphysics says:
> ***Like attracts like.***

Religious teaching tells us:
> ***The more we give, the more we receive.***

Spiritual principles talk about how:
> ***Giving creates a vacuum, a powerful attracting force, waiting – wanting – to be filled.***

Systems theory tells us:
> **What affects a part affects the whole.**

Holistic thinking leads us to conclude:
> **Whatever affects us, affects those around us, and thus the world in which we live.**

All these declarations are simply other ways of stating the Universal Principle:
> **We are One. We can only give to ourselves.**

What's most important to realize is giving comes first. Giving precedes receiving. Waiting until we have more, something extra to share, is not the way Life works.

> **Give a person a big, warm, welcoming smile and most will smile back.**
> **Wait for others to smile first, and far less cheer will come your way.**

Giving creates a void, a vacuum, that attracts what will nourish, restore and reward. A Tithe, a gift of love freely given without expectation of return, acts like a powerful magnet. The greater the magnitude of a free-will love offering, the more powerful the attracting force created.

This is Universal Law. This is how energy works.

> **The more we give, the more we get, the more we have to give again.**

>   And

> **The more we help create a better world, the more we benefit from the better world in which we live.**

As saints and sages have known for thousands of years:

Everything we give is always a gift to ourselves.

Thus...

It makes sense to share more instead of less.
It makes sense to make tithing a way of life.

Unfortunately, a surprising number of people find it difficult to be generous. Studies show that the higher one's income, the less of a percentage that person gives. A commitment to tithe demands major shifts in how we think and act. It takes time to change our attitudes and release the fears that hold us back. Remember, progress is faster and easier when we applaud and celebrate each new step we take.

Generosity is determined by our willingness to share what we have. It is our intent, not the gift itself, that speaks our gratefulness. You alone determine if a tithe is deserved and what it should be.

It helps to realize that our resources are not limited to money or material things. We can give our time, share our skills, lend an ear, help with tasks, pass on compliments, express love. Simply let your imagination suggest what's appropriate.

As you explore making tithing a way of life, be aware that your ability to receive is equally important. Tithing is a reciprocal process. In order for the process to complete itself, you must accept a gift in return for your tithe. To better understand the promise "As you give, so shall you receive," keep these basic principles in mind:

The return gift may not happen right away.
> **It happens when the time is right.**

It isn't necessarily a direct reciprocal relationship.
> **It often comes from unexpected sources.**

You may not recognize the gift for what it is.
> **It will be just what you need.**

It won't happen if you aren't willing to receive.
> **Acceptance is an essential part of giving.**

A final important thought: Wanting to be fair, most of us try to determine the monetary value of the gifts we receive. Seldom are such estimates accurate.

> **How much we tithe should be based on how much we benefited from the gift, nothing else.**

Sometimes it's not until after the fact that we realize just how much or how well we have been served.

> **It's never too late to make up for what we didn't – or couldn't – give earlier.**

Bless you for all you share. May your heartfelt generosity be quickly replenished and multiply.

Copyright @ 1997 & 2008 Ann McGill – Midwife of Consciousness
You may freely duplicate and distribute this information
as long as it contains this copyright information
and is given away free of charge.

An attractive, single-page pamphlet has been created for this purpose. See www.MiraclesMadeEasy.com to download.

Appendix B
Highly Recommended Books

Boone, J. Allen. *Kinship with All Life: Simple, Challenging, Real-Life Experiences Showing How Animals Communicate with Each Other and with the People Who Understand Them.*

The true story about a dog called Strongheart and his remarkable ability to communicate. If you enjoy a mix of humor, astonishment and reality, you'll find this a quick, fun read.

Bristol, Claude M. *The Magic of Believing.*

In this book, considered a classic, Bristol reveals how to achieve your potential.

Gawain, Shakti. *Creative Visualization*

This book teaches how to use imagery as a means of focusing on what you want and how to bring your desires into being.

Peirce, Penney. *The Intuitive Way: A Guide to Living from Inner Wisdom.*

This clear, well-written book provides a step-by-step process for opening yourself up to listening deeply.

Ray, Sondra. *I Deserve Love: How Affirmations Can Guide You to Personal Fulfillment.*

This how-to book examines affirmations as related to love, sexuality, forgiveness and more.

Remele, Patricia. *Money Freedom: Finding Your Inner Source of Wealth.*

Using money and abundance as a framework to teach personal growth and metaphysical principles, this book shows how unconscious thoughts undermine intentions, and how to change them.

Sinetar, Marsha. *Do What You Love, The Money Will Follow: Discovering Your Right Livelihood.*

This book offers guidelines to following the path of your heart and trusting the Universe to support your goals.

Wright, Machaelle Small. *Behaving as if the God in All Life Mattered.*

A remarkable woman's struggle to survive unusual difficulties as a teenager, followed by learning how to communicate with the invisible forces of nature.

Bibliography

Bach, Richard. *Illusions: The Adventures of a Reluctant Messiah.* 3rd Edition. New York: Delta, 1998.

Dyer, Dr. Wayne W. *You'll See It When You Believe It – The Way to your Personal Transformation.* Sag Harbor, NY: Bookman Press, 1989.

Hawken, Paul. *The Magic of Findhorn.* London: Foyles Group, 1976.

Appendix C
Highly Recommended Spiritual Teachers

Robert Adams
At age 14, during a math test, Robert experienced a spontaneous awakening. Soon thereafter he traveled to India, where he remained for the last three years of Ramana Maharshi's life. *Silence of the Heart,* one of my favorite books, is available at www.Amazon.com.

Amma
Even in early childhood, Amma displayed signs of her calling to ease suffering in the world. Known as the "Hugging Saint," she travels the globe spreading love through direct transmission. Amma has accomplished an amazing number of good works: building hospitals, creating housing and supporting disaster relief, schools and more. Learn more about Amma at www.Amma.org.

Tom Carpenter
For a long time, Tom's logical mind rejected as rampant imagination his conversations with Jesus, in which he received answers to questions he asked. Finally, he received undeniable proof that he really could tap into the Universal Mind. Tom became a teacher of *A Course in Miracles* and wrote *Dialogue on Awakening*, available at www.Amazon.com.

Gangaji
A student of H.W.L. Poonja, Gangaji's teaching focuses on the central tenet of Advaita Vedanta, that we are not our bodies, nor our minds, but pure awareness forever free. Articulate and clear, Gangaji conducts *Satsang* meetings around the world. You can access her schedule or order her books at www.Gangaji.org.

Ramana Maharshi
At age 16, Ramana experienced himself as dying. Diving into the experience rather than fearing and denying it, he realized the Truth of his Divine Nature. Considered one of the 100 most important people of the 20th century, Ramana introduced "Self Inquiry" as a path to enlightenment. His lineage includes Papaji, Gangaji and Robert Adams. You can explore his teachings at www.SriRamanaMaharshi.org.

H.W.L. Poonja
Known the world over as Papaji, this enlightened being – who laughed a lot and loved to play cricket – helped thousands to awaken to their True Nature. He was 8 years old when he experienced his first awakening and became fully enlightened when he first visited Ramana Maharshi some 25 years later. He wrote *The Truth Is* and *Wake Up and Roar*, available at www.Poonja.com or Amazon.com.

Appendix D
Highly Recommended Service Providers

Dianne Adams – *Astrologist*
Gain the most from your life's unique journey. Be aware of your gifts, recognize potentially compatible partners and take advantage of cycles of growth and change. It's so much easier to make wise decisions and take appropriate action when you allow yourself to be guided by Dianne's keen intuition and astrological knowledge. Private readings for individuals and businesses, in person or by phone. For contact information and a free newsletter see www.SpiritinMatters.com.

Teri-E Belf – *Success Coach and Coach Trainer*
Living the principles she teaches, Teri-E has created an extraordinarily meaningful, purposeful life. She coaches and trains coaches world-wide through Success Unlimited Network (SUN). Her books *Coaching With Spirit* and *Facilitating Life Purpose* provide valuable information for coaches and aspiring coaches. For information about coaching, ICF-accredited coach training / certification and spiritual exploration, contact Teri-E at 703-716-8374; coach@belf.org; www.belfcoach.com www.successunlimitednet.com.

Grey, Carol Hansen – *Empowerment Consultant*
The common thread to Carol's varied interests is teaching self-empowerment. Her *Lighten Up* CD teaches a powerful 5-minute-a-day self-love technique that produces profound results. Her *Free Yourself from Fear* CD shows you how to transform limiting thoughts and feelings instantly. As a graphic artist and web developer she helps clients to more fully express themselves. You can learn more at www.CarolHansenGrey.com and www.OpenHeart.com.

Beth Hampton – *Spiritually Oriented Psychotherapist*
Well versed in the teachings of *A Course in Miracles*, Ramana Maharshi and Eckhart Tolle, Beth offers spiritual direction through private sessions, group meetings and overnight retreats at her beautiful home and gardens in Manassas, VA. Psycho-spiritual counseling, spiritual discussion groups and retreats; 703-243-8199.

Pam McDonald, MSW – *Holistic Psychotherapist*
Highly intuitive, loving and gentle, Pam facilitates the healing of inner wounds and the activation of hidden strengths. A seasoned Reiki Master, her gifts as an energetic healer speed the process tremendously. Individual and group therapy, workshops, energy healing and Reiki training; 301-371-3228; Pmmcdonald1@verizon.net.

Ann McGill – *MidWife of Consciousness*
Quantum-leap change with the utmost joy, speed and ease is the hallmark of Ann's work. As you break free of what's holding you back and awaken to the beautiful truth of who you really are, you release a powerful force for achieving what's truly possible. Private consulting and group conversations by phone and in person; public speaking; 703-262-7757; MidWife@AnnMcGill.com; www.AnnMcGill.com.

Frances Oliver – *Transformation Coach & Professional Organizer*
Combining her passions and skills as a transformational coach and professional organizer, Frances gently leads you through the process of creating greater peace and order in your life. And she is truly a joy to work with! Coaching by phone, public speaking; 541-488-2336; info@soulofsimplicity.com; www.soulofsimplicity.com.

Toni Talentino – *Spiritual Guide*
Toni's purpose in life is to teach Fun & Frolic. Spiritually grounded, metaphysically informed, she adds joy and laughter to the process of learning how to create the kind of life you really want to live. Her coaching takes place in a cocoon of unconditional loving acceptance as she asks astute questions that bring you to ever greater clarity. One-on-one coaching, available by phone; 301-622-0966.

About Ann McGill

My good fortune begins with three beautiful daughters, two unique sons-in-law and a super special grandson. I live in a picturesque planned community near our nation's capital, close to a huge park along the Potomac River that I use as my outdoor office, meditation center and personal gym.

I love driving around in my polka-dotted car, blowing bubbles out the back, spreading joy and laughter wherever we go. If you see us, be sure to honk and wave.

Contact Information

Snail Mail: Ann McGill
P. O. Box 9302
Reston, VA 20195

Email: MidWife@AnnMcGill.com

Websites: www.MiraclesMadeEasy.com
www.JoyCar.org
www.AnnMcGill.com

*Miracles Made Easy
is offered as a
Gift of Love.*

*My thanks to all who
pass on the information
so that many more
may benefit.*

www.ingramcontent.com/pod-product-compliance
Lightning Source LLC
Chambersburg PA
CBHW061444040426
42450CB00007B/1211